# Radical Ambivalence

STUDIES IN THE CATHOLIC IMAGINATION:
THE FLANNERY O'CONNOR TRUST SERIES

*Edited by Angela Alaimo O'Donnell, Ph.D., Associate Director,*
*The Francis and Ann Curran Center for American Catholic Studies*

SERIES ADVISORY BOARD

Jill Baumgaertner, Wheaton College (Emeritus)
Mark Bosco, SJ, Georgetown University
Una Cadegan, University of Dayton
Michael Garanzini, SJ, Fordham University
Richard Giannone, Fordham University (Emeritus)
Paul Mariani, Boston College (Emeritus)
Susan Srigley, Nipissing University, Canada

# Radical Ambivalence

Race in Flannery O'Connor

ANGELA ALAIMO O'DONNELL

Fordham University Press
NEW YORK   2020

Copyright © 2020 Fordham University Press

All rights reserved. No part of this publication may be reproduced, stored in a retrieval system, or transmitted in any form or by any means—electronic, mechanical, photocopy, recording, or any other—except for brief quotations in printed reviews, without the prior permission of the publisher.

Fordham University Press has no responsibility for the persistence or accuracy of URLs for external or third-party Internet websites referred to in this publication and does not guarantee that any content on such websites is, or will remain, accurate or appropriate.

Fordham University Press also publishes its books in a variety of electronic formats. Some content that appears in print may not be available in electronic books.

Visit us online at www.fordhampress.com.

Library of Congress Cataloging-in-Publication Data

Names: O'Donnell, Angela Alaimo, author.
Title: Radical ambivalence : race in Flannery O'Connor / Angela Alaimo O'Donnell.
Description: First edition | New York : Fordham University Press, 2020. | Series: Studies in the Catholic imagination: the Flannery O'Connor Trust series | Includes bibliographical references and index.
Identifiers: LCCN 2020000615 | ISBN 9780823288243 (hardback) | ISBN 9780823287659 (paperback) | ISBN 9780823288250 (epub)
Subjects: LCSH: O'Connor, Flannery—Criticism and interpretation. | Race relations in literature. | O'Connor, Flannery—Political and social views.
Classification: LCC PS3565.C57 Z81255 2020 | DDC 813/.54—dc23
LC record available at https://lccn.loc.gov/2020000615

Printed in the United States of America

22 21 20   5 4 3 2 1

First edition

for Joseph Viscomi and Richard Giannone

Contents

| | | |
|---|---|---|
| | List of Abbreviations | ix |
| | Introduction: Two Minds | 1 |
| 1 | "Whiteness Visible": Critical Whiteness Studies and O'Connor's Fiction | 13 |
| 2 | Race, Politics, and the Double Mind: Flannery's Correspondence versus O'Connor's Fiction | 36 |
| 3 | Theology, Religion, and Race: Constant Conversion and the Beginning of Vision | 70 |
| 4 | "Africanist Presence" and the Role of Black Bodies | 97 |
| 5 | The Failure and Promise of Communion | 125 |
| | Acknowledgments | 145 |
| | Works Cited | 149 |
| | Index | 155 |

Abbreviations

Published Primary Works

CS      Flannery O'Connor, *The Complete Stories*
CW      Flannery O'Connor, *The Collected Works*
HB      Flannery O'Connor, *The Habit of Being*
MM      Flannery O'Connor, *Mystery and Manners*

Document Collections

Emory   Flannery O'Connor Letters, Stuart A. Rose Manuscript, Archives, and Rare Book Library, Emory University, Atlanta, Georgia
GCSU    Flannery O'Connor Collection, Ina Dillard Russell Library, Georgia College and State University, Milledgeville, Georgia

Radical Ambivalence

# Introduction: Two Minds

> I hope that to be of two minds about some things is not to be neutral.
> —FLANNERY O'CONNOR, LETTER TO ELIZABETH HESTER, MAY 4, 1957 (HB 218)

Flannery O'Connor's first published story, "The Geranium," written in 1946 when she was a student at the Iowa Writer's Workshop, tells the story of a displaced elderly white southerner named Dudley who suffers from homesickness after moving to the alien urban environment of New York City to live with his daughter. Much afflicts Dudley, but the circumstance that leads to his final devastation is a humiliating encounter with a black neighbor who offers assistance to the old man as he stumbles his way up the stairs of their apartment building and in the process condescends to him, addressing him as "old-timer" and speaking "in a voice that sounded like a nigger's laugh and a white man's sneer" (*CS* 12). Juxtaposed to this encounter is Dudley's sentimental reminiscence about his idyllic life back home hunting and fishing with his black companion, Rabie, "a light-footed nigger," who would "do his running for him" (*CS* 11), call him "boss," help him sniff out a covey of birds and find the best fishing spots on the river. Physically and psychically shaken by the black man's treatment of him, Dudley finally returns to his seat in the apartment he occupies with his daughter, filled with despair at the brave new world he finds himself in. As the story concludes, he grieves for himself and for the loss of the Jim Crow life he has led and loved, the comfortable dispensation of white privilege and black submission.

Eighteen years later, as O'Connor lay dying from lupus, she worked on her last story, "Judgement Day." It was a revision of "The Geranium." This would be the fourth version of the story and would be published as the final piece in the posthumously issued collection, *Everything That Rises Must Converge*. In this retelling of the tale, Old Dudley, now renamed

Tanner, also reminisces about his long and now lost relationship with his black companion, renamed Coleman—only their kinship is characterized as more intense and foundational, as if Coleman were "a negative image of himself" (CS 538–39), yet it is one wherein Tanner insists the black man "treat him like he was white" (CS 539). Also in this version of the story, the protagonist has a fateful encounter with a black neighbor in the apartment building—only this time it is Tanner who condescends to the neighbor, addressing the well-dressed man as "Preacher," assuming he hails from South Alabama, and inviting him on a fishing expedition according to the southern black/white dispensation: "I thought you might know somewhere around here we could find us a pond" (CS 544). The encounter in the revised story proves even more devastating than in the original version as the neighbor seethes with an "unfathomable dead-cold rage" at this open display of the old man's racism. At the end of the story Tanner is dead, if not actually murdered by the black man he insulted, assaulted by him as the old man suffers a stroke.

This tale of racial alienation and violence bookends O'Connor's career. It is one she returned to again and again, presumably with the goal of getting the story right, both in terms of refining her craft and in terms of creating greater nuance in her handling of the theme of race. The story features a number of O'Connor's signature themes—including displacement, the passing of a moribund social order, moral blindness, and the loss of identity—but the central focus is the fraught and volatile relationship between African Americans and whites. It is race that dominates the consciousness of Old Dudley and Tanner—the loss of the black companion against whom each man defined himself as white, the violation of the simple yet deeply embedded code by which whites and blacks had lived in the South for a century and more, the leveling of the hierarchy that gave permission for the domination of one group of human beings over another. It is also significant that the fate of the protagonist becomes more dire as the story evolves and O'Connor explores more fully and deeply the investment of white culture in a racist dispensation. Tanner does not know how to live in the world he encounters, one in which his very identity is threatened and rendered uncertain. While it is true that he is killed by the black man whom he insults, it is also arguable that he is killed by the political and social forces that no longer permit slavery or its contemporary vestige in the de jure enforcement of racial domination in the form of Jim Crow. In the course of O'Connor's tale, which also functions as social critique and commentary, it is not just a man who dies but also a way of life and a way of thinking about black/white relations.

It is no accident that these two stories should be O'Connor's first and last. Even though race is not typically the primary focus in her thirty-one stories and two published novels, from beginning to end race is a constant presence in O'Connor's work, just as surely as African Americans were a constant presence in the lives of southern whites in the 1950s and 1960s. While the subject of race has been noted and explored by a number of literary critics over the decades, beginning in the 1970s and continuing to the present, there is, as yet, no sustained treatment of O'Connor's portrayal of the problem of race. This study seeks to fill this gap by approaching O'Connor's fiction from a number of disciplinary perspectives, engaging the link between race and religion, as well as links between race and politics and race and culture. In addition, the application of concepts from the fields of racial formation theory and critical whiteness studies to O'Connor's work helps to focus attention where O'Connor clearly wanted it to be, as evidenced in many of her stories: on the ways in which racism and a racist caste system shape (and misshape) white people, its inventors and perpetrators. In O'Connor's world, those who stand to gain the most from the system suffer from it in ways they are unaware of, and rooted within the system are the seeds of its destruction.

This study explores the complexity, the development, and the limitations of O'Connor's vision with regard to race as embodied in her writings, and the radical ambivalence in which her attitudes toward race are rooted. This ambivalence manifests itself in O'Connor's correspondence (as is evident in the epigraph to this Introduction) as well as in her fiction. Accordingly, the study will examine the relationship between the ideas about race expressed in her letters and those represented in the stories. In addition, the study necessarily has a biographical dimension. As Hilton Als states, "O'Connor's most profound gift was her ability to describe impartially the bourgeoisie she was born into, to depict with humor and without judgment her rapidly crumbling social order" (119). O'Connor did not shy away from portraying the evil human beings are capable of, and one of the reasons she was able to see it so clearly in her fellow creatures is that she was subject to it, as well. When she depicts the racist thoughts of Ruby Turpin in her story "Revelation" or of Julian's mother in "Everything That Rises Must Converge," she is on familiar turf—not only because these are the ideas freely espoused by her family and acquaintances, but because she herself, as a white person living in the pre–civil rights era in the American South, has likely entertained them as well. This propensity becomes most evident in O'Connor's letters, particularly those she exchanged with friends and fellow writers Maryat Lee and Elizabeth Hester. Though many of these are included in Sally Fitzgerald's collection of O'Connor's letters, *The Habit of Being*, and in the *Collected Works*, some have remained unpublished and are available only in the Georgia College and State University Library and Emory University Library special collections. Reading through these letters, it is not difficult to imagine why they were not selected for publication by Fitzgerald, a dear friend of O'Connor's, or by her mother Regina Cline O'Connor, who controlled the estate until her death at the age of ninety, since O'Connor demonstrates attitudes that are hard to describe as anything but patently racist. Paul Elie, in *The Life You Save May Be Your Own: An American Pilgrimage*, summarizes the content of the letters. Despite O'Connor's depiction of the evils of racism in her stories, "There is the word 'nigger' running through the correspondence. There are quips about blacks, offered again and again as punch lines. There is, in the letters, a habit of bigotry that grows more pronounced as O'Connor's fiction, in the matters of race, grows more complex and profound—a habit that seems to defy the pattern of her art" (327).

The conundrum Elie presents is further complicated by the fact that at times, even in stories wherein O'Connor is consciously trying to convey a vision of racial egalitarianism, there are elements of the story that suggest otherwise (a point demonstrated in the analysis of "The Artificial Nigger," for instance, in Chapter 4). As Nicholas Crawford argues in his study of race in O'Connor's stories, "Although her feelings on race were complex and perhaps not entirely accessible even to her, they are nonetheless deeply and ambiguously embedded in her fiction" (9). It is this inconsistency with regard to O'Connor's ideas about race that Elie describes, this ambiguity Crawford notes, and the radical ambivalence they are both grounded in, that this study addresses.

## The Unpublished Letters: A Fresh Resource

My original research into these unpublished letters has been enlightening to me, both as a longtime reader and teacher of O'Connor's work and as a biographer and critic. Like many O'Connor scholars, I knew that the letters existed and also knew something of their tenor and content. But visiting the special collections and reading the actual words O'Connor penned, I felt both shaken and challenged. They present the reader with the proverbial smoking gun, offering clear evidence of O'Connor's deep ambivalence about the place of African Americans in society, her disapproval of desegregation, and her dislike of black people. (Granted, my response to this evidence of O'Connor's unsavory attitudes regarding race is likely shaped by the fact that I am socialized as white. People of color, who live a different reality with regard to the pervasiveness of white racism, would likely find this less surprising.)

In addition to being shaken by O'Connor's bald statements reflecting clearly racist views, I was deeply troubled by the realization that the letters in *The Habit of Being* and in the *Collected Works* have been bowdlerized, stripped of many references to "niggers" and descriptions of civil rights–related events that force readers to see O'Connor is a less than flattering light. Many of these omissions are made from the letters without benefit of ellipses, so the unsuspecting reader has no idea that any words, phrases, or sentences are missing. I suddenly understood that I could not trust the letters I had previously regarded as faithful record of O'Connor's private thoughts. Something I had been aware of in an abstract, intellectual way had now become clear in an experiential way.

As I mentioned, this discovery was disappointing, but it was also stirring—stirring because I anticipated that making O'Connor's statements public would help readers and scholars to understand her work and her life more fully. Though the O'Connor estate has historically been hesitant to allow the letters to be quoted by previous editors (including Sally Fitzgerald), biographers, and scholars (as evidenced by notes that appear in their publications which state clearly that all references to the letters will be paraphrased), I am glad and grateful to acknowledge that permission to quote from these letters has been granted for this project, making passages from the letters available to many readers for the first time.

Given the nature of some of the passages in the letters, the previous refusal to give permission to quote from them is understandable. The motivation was surely the desire on the part of O'Connor's family to protect her legacy and reputation. The sympathetic way of seeing this protectiveness is that it may seem unfair to publish a writer's words written in private letters meant for private consumption and to do so posthumously, since she cannot defend herself or her views. Every person is entitled to privacy, whether she is a celebrated writer or not. In addition, it might be argued, O'Connor was a person of her time and circumstance, and it may seem unfair to take her words out of their historical context and to judge her in accord with a more recent, more socially progressive perspective. This view, of course, ignores the value of truth-telling, and it is a happy turn of events for O'Connor readers and scholars that the estate has adopted a new perspective and a generous policy. Seeing O'Connor's letters in their entirety, including the excerpted passages, set beside her stories, many of which attest to the dignity of African Americans and the ugliness of racist whites, demonstrates that it is possible to be of two minds—indeed, of several minds—at the same time, particularly when it comes to an issue that cuts close to the bone, as the civil rights movement did for southerners.

In a letter to Elizabeth Hester excerpted in the epigraph to this Introduction, O'Connor acknowledges her deep ambivalence (a word whose root, "ambi," meaning "both," suggests double-mindedness) with regard to matters of racial justice and the supposedly dangerous and disruptive efforts being made to achieve it: "I hope to be of two minds about some things is not to be neutral" (*HB* 218). This simple statement speaks elegantly to the conflict O'Connor felt regarding the problem of race in America. Rather than appearing "neutral" toward the great question of her era, O'Connor "hopes" to be on the right side of history; however, fidelity requires that she be true to her instincts, her cultural formation, and her inburnt beliefs. This inner conflict between aspirational hope and the reality of her own experience is the root and source of the inconsistencies of attitude evident in O'Connor's writings with regard to race, manifesting an ambivalence that marks her as flawed and deeply human. There is something salutary in the project of seeing a writer's genius (a quality that sets her apart from ordinary human beings) set beside her human limitations (a condition we all share) and discovering what the one has to do with the other. As W. B. Yeats once famously noted, "We make out of the quarrel with others, rhetoric, but of the quarrel with ourselves, poetry" (20). O'Connor's "poetry," in the form of her fiction, is the practical result of her ambivalence. A creative mind is a conflicted one, and O'Connor's writings, and particularly her letters, enable us to see the nature of that conflict as well as its generative effects.

## The Critical Landscape

A quick overview of the critical landscape reveals that critics have approached the difficult issue of the apparent racism embodied in O'Connor's writings in a variety of ways over the decades. Julie Armstrong, in her essay "Blinded by Whiteness: Revisiting Flannery O'Connor," offers a helpful summary of the major developments in the critical conversation (77). Melvin G. Williams, among other critics writing in the 1970s, sees telltale evidence of O'Connor's racist views in her stories, lamenting that black characters in her fiction exist "only to precipitate a white reaction" (132). Claire Kahane continues this line of interrogation of O'Connor's fiction, arguing that though she did extend stereotypes of her black characters "beyond their predictable boundaries," she still remained unable to imagine the interiority of African Americans and, therefore, remained trapped by the prejudices of her own culture (187, 198). Janet Egleson Dunleavy, writing in 1985, sees greater nuance in O'Connor's attitudes, tracing the pattern of treatment of African Americans in light of historical events in her fiction from her earliest stories (written just after World War II) to her last stories (written the same year as the Civil Rights Act of 1964). Doreen Fowler, in a number of studies of O'Connor's fiction published from the 1990s to the present, considers her work in light of several theoretical perspectives, arguing that O'Connor, fully aware of the difficulty of portraying the complexities of the South's racial realities, critiques the assumptions of her era with regard to race by deconstructing "the myth of white male superiority" and suggesting that "the difference between black and white is a matter of language and social construction" ("Deconstructing Racial Difference" 22). Ralph Wood, also writing in the 1990s to the present, takes a primarily theological approach to the problem, acknowledging that O'Connor was not sympathetic to the civil rights movement and that she often made "uncharitable" (97) remarks about African Americans in her letters, but claiming that O'Connor's fiction offers "the antidote to racism" ("Where Is the Voice Coming From?" 92). In O'Connor's view, according to Wood, such an intractable human problem can be solved only by God.

Each of these critical positions has some merit, and each provides the reader with a legitimate vantage point from which to consider the conundrum of O'Connor's contradictory ideas about race. As Armstrong goes on to point out in her essay, a perspective that has not been adequately explored is that of critical whiteness studies (81), a branch of critical race theory that examines the concept of whiteness, its origins, implications, and consequences for the culture in which it operates. Critical whiteness studies highlights the ways in which society is structured and governed by ideas and assumptions about race and reveals a system of privilege and privation that rewards whites and punishes nonwhites. By redefining racism as "a structural relationship based upon the subordination of one racial group by another" (Omi and Winant, Second Edition 157) rather than a set of attitudes or behaviors exhibited by people of one race toward those of another, one begins to realize that a person can be racist purely by virtue of participation in a racist system. As a white person in the pre–civil rights South, O'Connor (along with the characters she created) enjoyed all of the privileges that come with being white and did so quite unconsciously, as is the case with the vast majority of white people. According to Ruth Frankenberg in *White Women, Race Matters: The Social Construction of Whiteness*, in order to understand one's role as a white person in a racist system, it is necessary to see whiteness as "a location of structural advantage, of race privilege . . . a standpoint from which white people look at [themselves], at others, at society" and involving "a set of cultural practices that are usually unmarked and unnamed" (1). They are "unmarked" and "unnamed" because whiteness is not racialized in the way that blackness is. Whites rarely define themselves in terms of their skin color in the way that people of color do as whiteness is regarded by our culture as the norm and blackness a deviance from that norm.

O'Connor's fiction often enabled her to escape the limitations of her white perspective. She was able to see the blindness and prejudices of her characters and to expose and critique their benighted racial attitudes. Seeing the limitations in her own attitudes and behaviors, however, was a more challenging enterprise. These limitations inevitably enter into her stories, as well, despite her best efforts. A few critics have used some of the principles of critical whiteness studies to characterize and delineate those limitations. Timothy P. Caron, assessing the diversity of critical approaches to O'Connor's treatment of race, argues that critics who discuss O'Connor's treatment of African Americans fall into two categories—the "True Believers," who see the world the way O'Connor saw it, as fallen, imperfect, and unable to be helped by programs of social justice advocated by the civil rights movement versus "The Apostates" who see O'Connor's theological stance as an obstacle to a sensitive and sympathetic portrayal of the plight of African Americans (138–39). Caron argues that O'Connor writes from a perspective of "theological whiteness" as well as "literary whiteness," in that her fiction excludes the perspective of black Americans who operate as "spiritual Step-n-fetchits, ushering her white characters toward their salvational moment" (163). John N. Duvall extends this idea, focusing on the ways in which O'Connor's black characters are drawn and the ways in which blackness is used to symbolize evil and spiritual darkness. In his 2008 book *Race and White Identity in Southern Literature,* he points out that the language and tropes that O'Connor inherits and uses are colored by race: "Following one of the deeply engrained binaries of western metaphysics, Christianity aligns whiteness with purity, while blackness figures humanity's fallen nature," an opposition that inevitably pervades O'Connor's fiction (63). Though O'Connor's art often constitutes a victory over her own prejudices, that victory is a partial one. Much as contemporary readers might wish to see the work of one of America's most brilliant writers as unadulterated by the destructive attitudes associated with racism, it is inevitably colored by the history and culture it has emerged from and seeks to portray.

Flannery O'Connor was, like many people of her own time and ours, a walking contradiction when it came to matters of race. She was not the only writer who wrestled with the legacy of slavery, racism, and Jim Crow in her native South and who expressed a complicated attitude toward attempts to ameliorate the conditions of African Americans. William Faulkner, for instance, wildly seesawed back and forth in his writings and statements on race, demonstrating a deep empathy with the African American characters who get caught up in the tragedy of racism in his fiction yet also making plainly racist statements. In an interview in 1956 with Russell Howe, he acknowledges that while he abhorred the injustices of segregation he equally abhorred the idea of the US government interfering with the right of southern states to deal with their race problems: "If it came to fighting I'd fight for Mississippi against the United States even if it meant going out into the street and shooting Negroes" (Meriwether and Millgate 261). This outrageous confession, famous in Faulkner studies, flies in the face of more moderate statements Faulkner made during this era—and even in the same interview—demonstrating an attitude that makes the study of Faulkner and race "a hellishly complex topic" (Polk 137). There is a robust literature devoted to exploring this deep fissure evident in Faulkner's view of race. The complicated nature of O'Connor's attitude (though it is never expressed quite so violently) deserves similar attention. Rather than try to deny, defend, or resolve her contradictions, it seems more fruitful to explore them, to discover and document the particular ways in which they manifest themselves in her writings. This study attempts to do just this, enabling readers to see the portrayal of race in her fiction from contemporary as well as historical perspectives, political as well as theological ones, so that we might better understand not only the forces O'Connor was subject to but also the forces that help to shape the work of artists in every era.

## Approach and Method

The study proceeds through a series of chapters, each of which explores O'Connor's work through a different lens. Chapter 1, "'Whiteness Visible': Critical Whiteness Studies and O'Connor's Fiction," summarizes the treatment of race in O'Connor criticism from the 1970s to the present, outlines some key concepts of racial formation theory and whiteness studies, and considers their potential relevance and application to O'Connor's work. The chapter includes a brief history of the idea of race, examination of the "color line" and the racial code observed by whites and blacks in the South, and exploration of O'Connor's attitudes toward that code as evident in some of her letters and in her representations of black characters in her stories. The chapter includes analysis of her first and last stories, "The Geranium" and "Judgement Day."

Chapter 2, "Race, Politics, and the Double Mind: Flannery's Correspondence versus O'Connor's Fiction," provides necessary background for the origins of O'Connor's ideas about race. It focuses on concepts of race O'Connor inherited, challenges to those ideas she may have encountered going to graduate school in Iowa and living in New York, and O'Connor's response to the events of the civil rights movement. This chapter includes discussion of O'Connor's correspondence, especially the letters exchanged between O'Connor and Maryat Lee and between O'Connor and Elizabeth Hester (both published and unpublished), and it considers the light they shed on O'Connor's attitudes. In assessing the inconsistency evident in O'Connor's discussion of race in the letters and in the stories, the chapter includes discussion of speech act theory, particularly Barbara Herrnstein Smith's differentiation between "natural" and "fictive" discourse. These considerations serve as foundation for an analysis of O'Connor's treatment of race in some of her early stories, including "The Geranium" (reprise), "The Barber," "Wildcat," and "The Coat."

Chapter 3, "Theology, Religion, and Race: Constant Conversion and the Beginning of Vision," considers the influence of theological concepts of race and the Church on O'Connor's thinking about race and the application of current theological studies of racism to O'Connor's work. This includes a review of the history of the Catholic Church's attitudes toward race and segregation, especially in the South, discussion of the influence of the theological visions of William Lynch and Teilhard de Chardin on O'Connor's thought, as well as consideration of theologian Brian Massingale's and M. Shawn Copeland's recent work on Catholic theological ethics and racial justice. The chapter also contains an analysis of "Revelation."

Chapter 4, "'Africanist Presence' and the Role of Black Bodies," taking its title and cue from Toni Morrison's seminal study of race in American literature, *Playing in the Dark: Whiteness and the Literary Imagination*, examines O'Connor's exploration of the essential role played by African Americans in the construction of a white consciousness. It also considers the work of womanist theologian M. Shawn Copeland on "enfleshing freedom" in which she meditates on the imaging of the black body in Western culture and its implications in the Christian Church. The chapter considers the difference between what anthropologist Mary Douglas refers to as "physical bodies" and "social bodies" and the ways in which these representations and perceptions of the body enter into O'Connor's work (73). The chapter includes analysis of "Everything that Rises Must Converge," "The Artificial Nigger," and "Judgement Day" (reprise).

Chapter 5, "The Failure and Promise of Communion," explores the theme of thwarted communion between the races that pervades O'Connor's correspondence and fiction. Her relentless interest in portraying the failure and the hope of such communion is evident in "The Enduring Chill" and in her novel *The Violent Bear It Away*, as well as in other stories. The chapter concludes with a brief summation of the primary findings of the study as a whole and argues that O'Connor's race-haunted work is a record of her commitment to trying to understand the complexity of the relationship between the races and to convey it faithfully.

As is evident in the preceding outline, this study explores O'Connor's work through a series of theoretical approaches and brings them into conversation with one another. Racial formation theory and critical whiteness studies constitute an important, but not an exclusive perspective. These ideas recur periodically in the course of the book to enrich the ensuing explorations that focus on the historical, political, theological, religious, and literary contexts that inform O'Connor's writing, but this study is not meant to be an extended analysis of all the implications of these racial theories in her fiction. My intention is to illuminate the role of race in O'Connor's work and to use a variety of sources to accomplish this in order to create a full spectrum of possibility.

The ultimate goal of this study is not to diminish the power, beauty, or authenticity of Flannery O'Connor's work. To the contrary, my hope is that it demonstrates the particular and inevitable limitations of her perspective with regard to race and the ways in which her art often enables her to qualify and renegotiate those limitations.

On a regular basis, in her letters and essays, O'Connor plainly acknowledges the limitations within which she must work as an artist; however, she also embraces that limitation as a salutary condition, one that grounds her vision and gives her permission to write about the world and the people she knows: "To call yourself a Georgia writer is certainly to declare a limitation, but one which, like all limitations, is a gateway to reality" (*MM* 54). O'Connor knows what she could write about with authority and what she could not. The latter category includes an understanding of the perspective of African Americans. When asked why "Negroes" do not figure more prominently in her stories, O'Connor explains, "I don't understand them the way I do white people. I don't feel capable of entering the mind of a Negro. In my stories they're seen from the outside. The Negro in the South is quite isolated; he has to exist by himself. In the South segregation is segregation" (Magee 59). No artist can be all things to all people, and to her credit, O'Connor doesn't try. And yet, it is her hope and expectation that her work, local and limited as it may be, will speak to readers in a universal way: "The writer operates at a peculiar crossroads where time and place and eternity somehow meet. His problem is to find that location" (*MM* 59).

O'Connor does, indeed, find that location—over and over again. The constantly growing appeal of O'Connor's work from generation to generation and across cultures attests to her remarkable ability to speak truth about the human condition, including our lamentable history and contemporary circumstance of the relationship between the races. Sometimes the work speaks in ways that she intends it to, while at others it speaks in ways that even this consummate artist and obsessive revisionist was not necessarily aware or in control of. In a televised interview of O'Connor conducted by Harvey Breit in 1955, O'Connor states, "A serious fiction writer describes an action only in order to reveal a mystery. Of course, he may be revealing this mystery to himself at the same time as he is revealing it to everyone else. He may not even succeed in revealing it to himself, but I think he must sense its presence at least" (Magee 9).

O'Connor's respect for the power of her craft and its potential to lead her to unfamiliar, uncharted, veiled places is clear. It is those veiled places this study explores, those unconscious moments of revelation that convey the fraught project of trying to speak about the desperately difficult subject of race. This study highlights the courage that it takes for a white southern writer to delve into this subject with a clear understanding of the possibility of failure and the courage that it took, when she did fail (as she did in her first story, "The Geranium"), to write it again and again and again—a process of revision and revelation that was brought to a halt only by her death. In a sense, O'Connor was working her way, story by story, toward a fuller understanding of the mystery of race. It is impossible to say where this process would have led her had her life and work not come to such an abrupt and premature end. Scholars and readers must work with what we have, the rich, troubled, and troubling fiction O'Connor left behind. It is my hope that this study situates O'Connor's work in our current contemporary cultural context and might help us to discover what it can teach us.

# 1 / "Whiteness Visible": Critical Whiteness Studies and O'Connor's Fiction

In her celebrated essay "Beyond the Peacock: The Reconstruction of Flannery O'Connor," African American novelist Alice Walker takes stock of O'Connor's contribution to Southern and American literature. Walker attests to feeling a strong affinity for her predecessor's work from her earliest reading of her, despite the fact that, as a white writer, O'Connor's fiction depicts the world from a white perspective. As a fellow southerner weary of fiction by white writers (Faulkner, Welty, and McCullers) "who seemed obsessed with a racial past that would not let them go" (51), Walker was grateful to discover that "*Essential* O'Connor is not about race at all, which is why it is so refreshing, coming, as it does, out of such a *racial* culture. If it can be said to be 'about' anything, then it is 'about' prophets and prophecy, 'about' revelation, and 'about' the impact of supernatural grace on human beings who don't have a chance of spiritual growth without it" (53; emphasis Walker's). Walker here notes the expansive nature of O'Connor's work, acknowledging that her characteristic concern is theological, focused on human beings and their relationship to the divine, rather than on the narrower subject of the social and political relationships created by America's racist history and culture. Walker's generous assessment of O'Connor's fictional world extends to her evenhanded portrayal of black characters, who seem as just as recognizably real—and just as "shallow, demented and absurd"—as their white counterparts. She credits O'Connor with creating characters, black and white alike, "whose humanity if not their sanity is taken for granted" (52). Far from being offended by the fact that O'Connor does not attempt to see the world from the perspective of African Americans, she admires O'Connor's restraint and better wisdom: "That she retained a certain distance (only, however, in her later, mature work) from the inner workings of her black characters seems to me all to her credit, since, by deliberately limiting her treatment of them to cover their observable demeanor and actions, she leaves them free, in the reader's imagination, to inhabit another landscape, another life, than the one she creates for them" (52).

What some critics would come to see as O'Connor's lack of sympathy and imaginative identification with African Americans (a critical view that will be more fully developed later), Walker sees as a sign of respect. The fact that O'Connor does not intrude on the lives of the black characters she creates is, according to Walker, "a kind of grace," a fine artistic instinct O'Connor is gifted with (52). Rather than insisting "on knowing everything, on being God," O'Connor gives African Americans in her stories privacy, agency, and freedom (52). Although O'Connor may devote less attention to her black characters, for Walker less constitutes more. Acknowledging the necessity of limitation, a practical reality that every fiction writer (herself included) must embrace, Walker suggests that this circumstance can be used advantageously. No writer can tell every story from every perspective. Instead, she must choose. O'Connor chose not to make race her primary subject, just as she chose not to allow the Civil War or the civil rights movement to loom large in her portrayal of the lives of southerners. As has been demonstrated by many critics writing before and after Walker, and as suggested by O'Connor herself in her letters and essays, O'Connor's interests lay elsewhere. "The topical is poison," she once wrote, and with few exceptions, she avoided directly addressing "the race thing" like the plague (*HB* 537).

Even so, despite her intentions not to dwell on race as the focal point of her stories, race and race relations pervade O'Connor's fiction. There would be no way to write about the world O'Connor occupied, and to write as she wrote, "hotly in pursuit of the real" (*MM* 171), without inclusion of an African American presence. Though race may be an accidental rather than an intentional presence (as Walker suggests), occupying the background rather than the foreground of her stories and novels, it is part of the texture of the social fabric portrayed in her fiction and lends her work the breadth and universality that genuinely great literature must have. In fact, race enters into the stories more often than O'Connor might intend it to in much the same way that words or ideas one might try to avoid speaking come out of one's mouth when one least expects them to, bringing to light what one might prefer to keep hidden. Like most human beings, O'Connor navigated a racially charged world, and like most white people living "in a social context where white people have too often viewed themselves as nonracial or racially neutral," she was frequently unaware of this (Frankenberg 1). African Americans have long known, as a result of four hundred years of participation in American culture, that there is no such thing as a non-racialized society, a fact that many white people are only gradually coming to learn. In the words of W. E. B. Du Bois, "The discovery of personal whiteness among the world's peoples is a very modern thing" ("The Souls of White Folk" 30).

## Critical Dissent

Written in 1975, Walker's essay is designed to be an appreciation of O'Connor's work rather than a sustained analysis or critique, an opportunity to come to terms with the elder writer's lifetime contribution after the posthumous publication of her *Complete Stories* and its garnering of the National Book Award in 1972, an unprecedented event in that the award had been given previously only to living authors. While Walker's respectful assessment of O'Connor's African American characters commends her conscious effort to work within her own limitations with regard to portraying the experience of black people, a number of literary critics were beginning to bristle at O'Connor's treatment of African Americans in her fiction. Melvin Williams's article published the following year, "Black and White: A Study in Flannery O'Connor's Characters," claims that her "Black characters are for the most part only 'issues' instead of people. . . . They never change, never are explored on a more than superficial level" (130). Williams objects to the very qualities Walker praises, namely, O'Connor's distance and detachment, and concludes by asserting that she affords her black characters "a separate-yet-unequal status," ironically echoing the language of the historic *Plessy vs. Ferguson* ruling that established segregation in 1896 and the *Brown vs. The Board of Education* ruling that overturned it in 1954, thereby implying some sympathy on the part of O'Connor with the old Jim Crow dispensation (132). Along similar lines, in 1978, Claire Kahane claims that "O'Connor appropriates the ready-made racial stereotype, using the Negro repeatedly as a metaphor of redemptive humility" (184), again accusing her of writerly behavior that Walker pointedly denies evidence of in her work.

This critique of O'Connor's black characters has continued to develop and proliferate in O'Connor studies, though there are plenty of critics who counter it as well, among them Toni Morrison, Ralph Wood, and Doreen Fowler, all of whom see in O'Connor a more complex and knowing treatment of race more in keeping with Walker's view. In her signature study *Playing in the Dark: Whiteness and the Literary Imagination,* published in 1992, Morrison credits O'Connor with making the canny connection between "Africanist 'othering'" and God's grace; the fact that that grace is received by white rather than black characters does not seem to trouble her, for it is the white characters who are most in need of it (14). Similarly, Wood in a 1994 article acknowledges that O'Connor almost certainly harbored racist attitudes, as evidenced in her letters (both published and unpublished), but argues (taking a characteristically theological tack) that her art does not, as her "racial sinfulness had been dissolved in an unbidden gift of artistic mercy" ("Racial Morals and Manners" 1082). More recently (2004), Doreen Fowler's defense of O'Connor is rooted in contemporary theory, arguing that O'Connor knowingly engaged, in some of her stories, in using her characters (black and white) to critique the cultural construction of identity conferred on human beings according to their race ("Writing and Rewriting Race" 31).

What are contemporary readers of O'Connor's fiction to do with this diversity of assessment and assertion regarding O'Connor's black characters and, by extension, her treatment of the topic of race? Is it helpful, necessary, or even possible to determine whether O'Connor or her work can be accurately described as racist? Is there some way to break out of the typical binary O'Connor critics tend to get trapped in, identifying her either as racist writer or secular saint, albeit one with warts?

## (Re)defining Black and White

One way of approaching these issues is to examine more closely and carefully some of the basic terms of the conversation—particularly *race*, *racism*, *blackness*, and *whiteness*. Consideration of the historical usage of these terms alongside more recent theories about nuances of meaning made available through racial formation theory and critical whiteness studies demonstrates their slipperiness and contingency and might enable us to understand and use them more precisely in exploring O'Connor's work.

In their groundbreaking study *Racial Formation in the United States from the 1960s to the 1980s*, sociologists Michael Omi and Howard Winant recount the history of the idea of race and race consciousness, identifying it as a modern phenomenon, originating with the European explorers who encountered in the New World people so different in appearance from themselves that they questioned whether they possessed souls and could belong to "the family of man" (58). The concept of race was used to justify appropriation of property (including bodies) belonging to natives, coercive labor, and extermination.

With the displacement of religion by science as a guide to understanding the physical world and the dedication of eighteenth- and nineteenth-century scholars to the study and ranking of humankind according to a racial hierarchy, race became a biological concept. This construction, of course, gave permission for horrific abuses, most notably the transatlantic slave trade, an inhuman practice that (mis)shaped Western culture and society for centuries and manifested itself in the pseudo-science of eugenics, fueling the rise of the Nazis in Germany and the Holocaust in the twentieth century. (The latter horrific event appears in various places in O'Connor's work, most notably in her story "Revelation," wherein the racist Ruby Turpin receives an inkling from her own subconscious that her nighttime habit of ranking people according to race and class has some connection to the railroad box cars and ovens used by the Nazis.)

Though the biological grounding of race has largely been disproven, this misperception endures, particularly in the popular imagination, and continues to fuel white supremacist ideology. Displacing these moribund theories is a sociohistorical concept of race. As such, "racial categories and the meaning of race are given concrete expression by the specific social relations and historical context in which they are embedded" (60). Accordingly, the concept of race and the values associated with it are not fixed or absolute but are, instead, relative and in a near-constant state of flux. They differ from society to society and culture to culture, as well as across time. According to Omi and Winant, "We tend to view race as something fixed and immutable—something rooted in 'nature.' Thus we mask the historical construction of race categories, the shifting meaning of race, and the crucial role of politics and ideology in shaping race relations. Races do not emerge full-blown. They are the results of diverse historical practices and are continually subject to challenge over their definition and meaning" (63–64).

In keeping with this view of race as a construction of culture, being *black* in the South during the 1950s and 1960s has a different valence than it would under other historical and social circumstances, and the same goes for being *white*. The meanings of those categories are most often determined by the socially dominant "race." Thus, it has been argued, slavery, lynching, and Jim Crow laws, among other oppressive measures and institutions, were social constructs designed to create an identity for black Americans as inferior to whites, and blacks were compelled to conform to the reigning *mythos*, resigning themselves to inhumane conditions, to living lesser lives and making do with lesser homes and schools, and fulfilling the stereotype whites had created for them. In *Making Whiteness: The Culture of Segregation in the South, 1890–1940*, Grace Elizabeth Hale addresses a key concept of critical whiteness studies that results from this dynamic, the performative nature of blackness and whiteness, employing the metaphor of an elaborate pantomime to describe the conditions of black white relations:

> The culture of segregation turned the entire South into a theater of racial difference, a minstrel show writ large upon the land. A black middle class was rising, with its unhinging of black race and class identities. . . . These threats made the ritualistic enactment of racial difference vital to the maintenance of white supremacy in the twentieth century. . . . Since southern black inferiority and white supremacy could not, despite whites' desires, be assumed, southern whites created a modern social order in which this difference would instead be continually performed. For whites, this performance, in turn, made reality conform to the script. (Hale 284)

As this narrative of the evolution of race relations in the South suggests, the *mythos* of white supremacy and black inferiority became a self-fulfilling prophecy. For African Americans to violate the rituals or refuse to play the role of blackness assigned to them invited the real threat of white retribution, often in the form of the grimmest of theatrical rituals, the publicly staged lynching (Hale 285).

This is the world O'Connor inherited, lived amid, and wrote about. However, none of this was fixed. The circumstances of the lives of black and white Americans were being called into question and altered in her lifetime by large-scale events (including World War II, Supreme Court rulings, and the civil rights movement) on a nearly day-by-day basis. These shifts were seismic in nature, particularly from the viewpoint of white southerners, and along with those changes the concept of what it meant to be black and white was changing. O'Connor is well aware of the contingent nature of race and race relations, as evidenced in her stories. The question her depictions of these changes raises—and often do not answer—is how she felt about those changes.

W. E. B. Du Bois once famously stated that "the problem of the Twentieth Century is the problem of the color-line" (*The Souls of Black Folk* 5). Where O'Connor stands, with regard to that line, is not entirely clear, as the dissonant voices of the critics and commentators cited above would suggest. In fact, it is arguable that O'Connor, herself, was not entirely sure of what she thought and how she felt about the reality of race in the America she lived in. This ambivalence is borne out in her correspondence. In an unpublished letter written to Maryat Lee, her liberal-minded friend of southern origins who was living and writing in New York City, on

May 3, 1964, a few months before the passage of the Civil Rights Act as well as a few months before her death, O'Connor writes, "You know, I'm an integrationist by principle & a segregationist by taste anyway. I don't *like* negroes. They all give me a pain & the more of them I see, the less and less I like them. Particularly the new kind" (GCSU; emphasis O'Connor's).

While it is necessary to consider the context of this letter, the fact that it was part of an extended correspondence between the two friends which amounted to a kind of role playing, with Maryat cast as the liberal northern intellectual and Flannery playing the role of the unreconstructed white southern racist (Gooch 335), it is nonetheless arresting and disturbing to hear O'Connor express a preference for segregation and admit to a personal dislike for African Americans. Like many southern whites who were her contemporaries, she admits on principle that integration is the just policy to pursue, but she does not like it. In addition, she seems certain that her antipathy for black people will only increase as their participation in the daily lives of white people increases. She sounds disconcertingly like one of her characters here, such as Julian's mother in "Everything That Rises Must Converge," who complains that integration means that blacks on the bus are now "thick as fleas" and acknowledges that black people should rise, "but on their own side of the fence" (*CS* 410, 408). While O'Connor is less extreme and, as Julie Armstrong notes, "more savvy about race than the characters she creates," passages such as this one suggest they are different more in degree than in kind (81). Again, O'Connor knows the thoughts of her white racist characters because she herself has entertained them. Such toxic animosities are in the air O'Connor breathes and, inevitably, become part of her way of seeing the world.

In her letter to Maryat Lee, O'Connor's reference to "the new kind" of "Negroes" she particularly dislikes bears some consideration. O'Connor may be referring to "The New Negro" described by Alain Locke in his historic anthology that takes the term as its title; published in 1925, Locke identifies an emerging trend among post–World War I African Americans of greater pride, assertiveness, and self-confidence as they make their way up North as part of the Great Migration, taking their destinies into their own hands. It's also possible she may be referring to the term as used by writers of James Baldwin's generation in reference to African Americans who are rising up and demanding their civil rights (*The Fire Next Time* 85). In either case, O'Connor makes it clear that she is not fond of black people of any stamp, and has marked out a particular dislike for the "kind" that has rejected the docile role African Americans have played for so long and become outspoken critics of the racial status quo, in word or in action. There is nothing in the rest of the letter to suggest that O'Connor is being anything less than brutally honest here. She chides Maryat for suggesting that a letter to the local newspaper objecting to racist practices might be effective, asserting (probably accurately) "that's not the way things get done in places like this." The rest of the letter goes on to describe O'Connor's recent hospitalization, the return of symptoms of lupus, and the new round of steroids being administered. She finally closes with teacherly writing advice to Maryat. The existence of such a letter—and others like it—might seem to be clear evidence of resistance to the claims of African Americans for equality and a deep-seated racism in O'Connor; however, she was also capable of writing a very different sort of letter to her friend William Sessions one year before this one in which she claims, "I feel very good about those changes in the South that have been long overdue—the whole racial picture. I think it is improving by the minute, particularly in Georgia, and I don't see how anybody could feel otherwise than good about that" (unpublished letter, qtd. in Wood, *Christ-Haunted South* 103; Gooch 337).

While the whiplash-inducing contrast between the sentiments expressed in these letters seems extreme, so were the times O'Connor was living in. Ralph Wood summarizes some of the events that were both symptoms and causes of the racial crisis southerners found themselves facing:

> [O'Connor's] publishing career [1952–1964] spans the same decade that brought the Supreme Court decision banning segregated education; the defiance of that ruling in the public schools of Little Rock and New Orleans, and at the universities of Alabama and Mississippi; the black bus and lunch counter boycotts in Montgomery and Greensboro; the bombing of the Negro Baptist churches in Birmingham; the slaying of civil rights workers in Mississippi and Alabama; the harassment of Clarence Jordan's interracial Koinonia Farms in O'Conner's own native state; the rise of Martin Luther King, Jr., as the nation's chief civil rights leader; and the massive protest march of blacks and whites from Selma to Montgomery. (*Comedy of Redemption* 107)

This long and yet partial list serves as a reminder of the massive social and political upheaval Americans—and especially southerners—were confronted with in their daily lives for a decade and more. While many southerners watched these events unfold and participated in them on the streets of their cities and towns, all were called to witness them through the agency of newspapers and, later, television coverage. A particularly horrific event Wood omits here is the lynching of Emmet Till in 1955 and his very public funeral. Young Till's brutalized body, exposed in an open casket funeral at his mother's insistence, became a powerful symbol of the violence innocent African Americans were subject to by whites, both historically and in the present moment. In that same year Rosa Parks refused to give up her seat on a bus, a bold gesture that launched the Montgomery boycott Wood mentions, a thirteen-month mass protest by African Americans that concluded with the Supreme Court ruling that segregation on public buses is unconstitutional. These unprecedented events have been captured in iconic photographs and film footage as part of the proud and shameful history of the civil rights movement in America, a large-scale social campaign that defied the institutionalized racism of American society, called into question all previous notions about the role of African Americans, and undoubtedly transformed the nation for the better. With the 20/20 hindsight history provides us with, it is difficult to imagine fair-minded, intelligent, decent people opposing what was clearly a great moral imperative, "the liberation of black people from their American, and particularly their Southern bondage" (*Comedy of Redemption* 107); nonetheless, history and human nature tell us otherwise.

Like many of her contemporaries, O'Connor was double-minded about the race question. Born and bred in the South, after her sojourn at Iowa in pursuit of her MFA, her writing residence at Yaddo in upstate New York, and her brief stay in New York City and at the Connecticut country home of Robert and Sally Fitzgerald, her illness forced her to return to her native ground—a return that meant, to some extent, readaptation to the culture that had produced her and was part and parcel of who she was. O'Connor understood that the changes that were taking place would alter the South forever, and that while assuredly this would translate into social gain, it would inevitably also mean loss of part of the South's identity. O'Connor had no desire to see Georgia morph into New York, a seemingly soulless place she had no taste for. "Everybody has to have a region, and I think in the South we're losing that regional sense," O'Connor once stated in an interview (Magee 30). Part of that regional identity she laments the loss of is "manners," the code of behavior that has characterized human contact, cultivated community, and preserved civility in the most challenging of situations:

> It requires considerable grace for two races to live together, particularly when the population is divided about fifty-fifty between them and when they have our particular history. It can't be done without a

> code of manners based on mutual charity.... When you have a code of manners based on charity, then when the charity fails—as it is going to do constantly—you've got those manners there to preserve each race from small intrusions upon the other. (Magee 103, 104)

Having grown up in the South, O'Connor was well schooled in the unspoken rules that governed social relations and interactions between blacks and whites. These rules were part of an elaborate code that addressed a broad spectrum of behavioral norms, ranging from strictures on whom you could befriend, date, and marry, to rules for verbal exchanges (subjects appropriate for conversation, forms of address, tone of voice), to the subtleties of body language (gestures, eye contact, the removal or retention of one's hat). From O'Connor's white perspective, the code she describes is advantageous to members of both races and bespeaks mutual respect; however, it is safe to say that it would be perceived differently from a black perspective.

James Baldwin, in his essay "They Can't Turn Back," written after a tour of the South during the civil rights era, speaks of the code as a dangerous minefield black men and women must navigate every day of their lives and imagines the danger he would incur in committing a social faux pas, such as extending his hand to a white woman in greeting, a gesture that would imply equality:

> On such small signs and symbols does the Southern cabala depend, and that is why I find the South so eerie and exhausting. This system of signs and nuances covers the mined terrain of the unspoken—the forever unspeakable—and everyone in the region knows his way across this field. This knowledge that a gesture can blow up a town is what the South refers to when it speaks of its "folkways." The fact that the gesture is not made is what the South calls "excellent race relations." It is impossible for any Northern Negro to become an adept of this mystery. (622)

In an essay on O'Connor and Baldwin, Carole K. Harris quotes this powerful statement, contextualizing it in the circumstances of Baldwin's first encounter with the "Southern cabala" in May 1960 upon landing at the Tallahassee airport and observing the interaction between a white woman and a black chauffeur, and she explores Baldwin's epiphany to good effect (4–5). As Baldwin's critique suggests, the code southerners keep has unequal value for blacks and whites, and the violation of that code—whether intentional or accidental—will result in unequal consequences. A "Negro" who violates the rules challenges the foundational ethos of the South, threatens the stability of society, and will inevitably be punished for his or her infraction. A more realistic and comprehensive version of the code would also include the horrific traditions of lynching and vigilante justice, the invisible but tangible pressure applied by the Ku Klux Klan, and the restrictions of Jim Crow. The supposedly civil code of manners O'Connor describes is, thus, undergirded by the threat of violence, a benign version of the enforced racial *mythos* or racial theater described by Grace Elizabeth Hale. O'Connor rarely acknowledges these violent aspects of the code in her correspondence, essays, or interviews, though interestingly, as we shall see, she does address them in her fiction in subtle ways—yet another manifestation of her doublemindedness. For her the code was a set of social conventions designed to keep the peace, but for African Americans the code was a prescriptive set of performative expectations, a form of enforced structural racism, and the price one paid for living in a racialized society in which they constituted the subordinate caste. As for the role played by white people, the very fact of participating in a racist system and benefiting from it, as white people do, makes them complicit. One need not be a card-carrying member of the KKK to be a racist. Here it is useful to recall the definition of racism endorsed by Omi and Winant and mentioned in the Introduction to this study, "a structural relationship based upon the subordination of one racial group by another" (Second Edition 157). This would seem to indict nearly all cultures at all times, and the social order of the South in the mid–twentieth century is among the more egregious examples of such a structural relationship.

## Blinded and Sighted by Whiteness

This brings us back to Alice Walker's original observation about O'Connor's fiction, especially her mature work, namely her reluctance to try to inhabit the personae of her black characters, a reluctance O'Connor herself, as we have seen, describes as an inability or limitation. In doing this, O'Connor grants these characters the freedom, according to Walker, to live an interior life other than the one the author determines for them. The quiet respect Walker finds in the stories is infinitely preferable to her, as an African American reader, to the paternalistic, omniscient role white writers typically choose to play in portraying blacks. Walker's point is a valid one. Even as she invades, ransacks, and exposes the corrupt imaginations of her white characters, O'Connor allows her black characters to retain an inviolable privacy. To paraphrase Hamlet, she does not pluck out the heart of their mystery, as the prince's supposed friends Rosencrantz and Guildenstern so unkindly endeavor to do (*Hamlet* 3.2.365–66). Instead, she describes their actions and outward demeanor, leaving their motivations ambiguous and, thus, full of suggestion and possibility. It is her white characters who are put on trial and, nearly always, found wanting. In fact, whiteness itself is put on trial in O'Connor's fiction, with all of its accompanying pride and prejudices, ugly superiority, and self-righteous evildoing. While O'Connor may not have 'liked' African Americans, according to her own admission, her stories suggest that she did not have much affection for white people *as* white people either. There is no doubt that O'Connor is sometimes "blinded by whiteness," as Julie Armstrong suggests in her essay on O'Connor and race (82–83); however, she is, at times, sighted by whiteness, as well. Her role as a writer was not to defend the behavior she saw in her fellow human beings but to eye it warily and portray and critique it with equal doses of honesty and compassion. This is what O'Connor means, in part, by her statement that a good fiction writer is "hotly in pursuit of the real" (*MM* 171). There is no doubt she is limited in that pursuit, as every writer must be—even her choice of the word "pursuit" suggests the striving for an end but not necessarily the achievement of it. O'Connor's limitation is her whiteness, and her whiteness also provides her with a vantage point from which to see the world—her world—in particular, the world inhabited and navigated by southern whites in the 1950s and 1960s.

O'Connor felt herself incapable of accommodating a black person's perspective in her work, but she knew African American presence was essential to her fiction, and she therefore sought to portray black characters in ways that were faithful to fact and that did not do violence to their autonomy. In her refusal to appropriate black consciousness, she demonstrates a sensitivity and nuance with regard to race that is often lacking in her correspondence.

As with any writer's work, O'Connor's bodies forth an amalgam of authorial intention and larger external forces that exert influence on her thinking and writing. Thus, it is possible for O'Connor to have made the artistic choices Alice Walker credits her with (and that O'Connor herself lays claim to) and at the same time for O'Connor to be the inheritor of and often unconscious participant in structures of racism and white privilege that shape and color her work. This "both/and" inclusive approach, rather than an "either/or" exclusive one, attempts to honor O'Connor's complexity—and the complexity of the imagination—by offering multiple angles and perspectives from which to consider her treatment of race without totalizing any one of them.

## From "The Geranium" to "Judgement Day"

It is fiction, in fact, that provides O'Connor with a proving ground for ideas that puzzled and perplexed her, an opportunity for her to wrestle with the competing claims of the traditional dispensation of race and privilege and the newly emerging dispensation of her own historical moment. As suggested in my Introduction, nowhere is that struggle more evident than in the writing and continual rewriting of her first and final stories, "The Geranium" and "Judgement Day."

In his study *Flannery O'Connor and the Mystery of Love,* Richard Giannone traces the development of O'Connor's Alpha and Omega story from its origins as her first published story (1946) and the title story of her Iowa MFA thesis (1947), through its second incarnation as "An Exile in the East," published posthumously in *The South Carolina Review* (1978), through its morphing into a third unpublished story titled "Getting Home," to its final form as "Judgement Day," which O'Connor sent off to her publisher, Robert Giroux, a month before her death (Giannone 233–54). The enduring pattern of the story that O'Connor pursues with increasing fidelity through each version is the desire for the protagonist, who is lost amid the alien culture of the North, to return home to his native South. Regarding her first story, O'Connor once confided in a letter to Maryat Lee that she could not write about being homesick herself (a feeling she was familiar with during her time in Iowa) as she was not an autobiographical writer by nature or impulse, but she could write about the homesickness of one of her characters (*HB* 204). Such an admission suggests a kind of surrogacy on the part of Old Dudley, the protagonist, who eventually morphs into T. C. Tanner in the final story. Although these men could not be more different from O'Connor, in terms of surface appearances and circumstances, the narrator in both stories views the world from his perspective and therefore shares vicariously in his journey, struggle, and revelation.

Both "The Geranium" and "Judgement Day" constitute explorations of what it means to be white in the cultures of the North and in the South and, to a lesser extent, what it means to be black. In her study "Writing and Rewriting Race," Doreen Fowler asserts that "race, as a marker of identity, is the central concern" of the two stories and suggests that O'Connor's obsessive revisions demonstrate her intention of exposing and exploring the cultural construction of an unstable racial identity (31). Both Old Dudley and Tanner yearn to return to the South and the privileges both characters enjoyed as white men. In particular, each wants to return to his African American companion and confidant, Rabie and Coleman, respectively, each of whom is, in some ways, a version of himself. Fowler frames her argument by reminding the reader of O'Connor's assertion in an unpublished manuscript that "the Negro, without losing his individuality, is a figure for our darker selves, our shadow side" (31). Thus, the reader is invited to see Dudley and Rabie, Tanner and Coleman, as pairs of doubles, doppelgängers, alternate versions of each other, each of whom is radically incomplete without the other.

Each man has come to New York of his own volition to live with his daughter but discovers that the city is inhospitable to life as he knows it and finds himself in a state of existential crisis. Both men are convinced that by going home again they will return to a state of psychic and spiritual health and wholeness, though each knows his days are numbered. The main motivation is not so much a return to a place as it is a return to his former self, emblematized by the African American companion he has left behind. Each white man longs for his black other. This longing becomes complicated when Dudley and Tanner meet African American men in the hallway of the apartment building in which they live. The encounters they have with these men challenge all of their assumptions about race and their respective places in the social order.

Though the two stories share a similar plot and explore similar terrain, the later incarnation of the story delves further into the psyche of its protagonist and portrays the relationship between whites and blacks as more deeply complex. Most critics see "The Geranium," in the words of Ralph Wood, as "a rather sentimental and moralistic allegory," which ultimately becomes, in the course of nearly twenty years of revision, "a penetrating piece of art" ("From Fashionable Tolerance to Unfashionable Redemption" 13). Old Dudley painfully discovers in his encounter with the friendly African American man in the hallway of his daughter's apartment building, who greets him with familiarity, calling him "Old Timer," helps him up the steps after he has fallen, and pats him on the back condescendingly, that the gulf that separates whites from blacks in the South has been breached, both physically and socially. Back home in the boardinghouse he lived in, Dudley occupied the upper rooms, while Rabie and his wife, Lutish, lived in the basement. Here in New York, a black man lives next door to him, occupying space literally and figuratively on the same level with him. All of this is too much for Dudley's fragile white psyche to bear. He returns to the apartment shaken and sickened, only to find that the geranium, the central symbol of the story, that used to sit in the window across the alley, a small element of natural beauty in the ugly urban landscape that offered some comfort to the homesick man, has crashed to the ground and now lies in the alley with its potted roots sticking up in the air, "a heavy-handed symbolic correlative to Dudley's shattered racial pride" (13).

In keeping with this view, the relationship between Old Dudley and Rabie is more simply rendered than the one shared by Tanner and Coleman. Rabie plays the role of the loyal "darkie" who happily navigates the river to find good fishing holes for Dudley and walks deftly beside him as they sneak up on a covey of birds, modeling a twentieth-century version of the master-slave relationship. In one telling scene Dudley recalls a time when the two went out hunting: Dudley, in his awkwardness, slipped and fell on a trail made slick by pine needles, dropping his gun (which promptly misfired) and scattering the birds into the air. Rabie, who had previously asked whether he might be the one to approach the birds, responded to Dudley's clumsy mismanagement of the hunt, "Dem was some mighty fine birds we let get away from us" (CS 11). Rabie's use of the pronouns "we" and "us" deflects blame from his white companion and implicates himself as somehow being at fault, even though it is clear to both men that Dudley is responsible for the lost opportunity. Though Rabie is more skilled and accomplished as a hunter and woodsman than Dudley, they both maintain the fiction that the opposite is true. Such are the dispensations white and black men live by; however, only the black man seems to be conscious of this, as he cautiously plays his role, while Dudley can afford to remain blissfully unaware. This is the traditional black/white dynamic Dudley misses and longs to return to.

Tanner, on the other hand, shares a more elemental relationship with Coleman—one that is less clear-cut, less reminiscent of the master/servant relation, and more like a bond of near-equals. Instead of the typical black/white binary one sees in "The Geranium," O'Connor builds into the story a racial continuum. As Fowler suggests, the new names of the characters signal a dialectical relationship, but one which is qualified. Tanner is described as "a yellow-faced scrawny white man," while Coleman, true to his name, is identified as "a large black loose-jointed Negro" (CS 537). Tanner may be perceived as white, but "only in relation to someone who is coal-black, his polar opposite" ("Writing and Rewriting Race" 32). This racial continuum is reflected later in the story in Tanner's description of the girlfriend of the African American neighbor he meets in the hallway as a "high-yeller, high-stepping woman with red hair" (CS 543). It is notable that the same intermediate color, "yellow," is associated both with the supposedly white protagonist and this supposedly black character. "Black" and "White" are relative terms in the world of "Judgement Day," thus blurring the distinctions the culture Tanner comes from insists upon.

This insistence upon the black/white binary is evident in the first meeting of Tanner and Coleman. When Coleman shows up at the sawmill in the middle of a pine forest where Tanner works as foreman to a crew of six black men, Tanner immediately recognizes him as a threat. Physically intimidating, "twice his own size," Coleman is also drunk and lazy, lying about the camp and sleeping in full view of his crew, a black man who the rest of the men recognize as an idler (*CS* 537). His influence is felt almost immediately when the six men decide to take their lunch break a full half-hour before noon. Tanner, who prides himself on being able to "handle niggers," knows he must do something to maintain the tentative control he has over his workers: he must figure out how to handle Coleman. He knows that his usual method, the wielding of his knife and threatening violence as he whittles away at a piece of wood (the latter activity a feint to hide his shaking hands, the result of a kidney problem), is risky, given Coleman's size and independent attitude, but he makes the attempt as it is the only one he knows. It is then that a remarkable thing happens: "His own penknife moved, directed solely by some intruding intelligence that worked his hands," and Tanner finds himself carving a pair of spectacles (*CS* 538). Both men seem surprised by the emergence of the spectacles from a block of wood, and they are even more surprised by the ritual that ensues. When Tanner hands the spectacles to the black man, telling him to put them on, Coleman complies:

> The Negro reached for the glasses. He attached the bows carefully behind his ears and looked forth. He peered this way and that with exaggerated solemnity. And then he looked directly at Tanner and grinned, or grimaced, Tanner could not tell which, but he had an instant's sensation of seeing before him a negative image of himself, as if clownishness and captivity had been their common lot. The vision failed him before he could decipher it. (*CS* 538–39)

Coleman's pantomime is a species of well-rehearsed theatricality in the South wherein African Americans are expected to play the role of the gullible fool before their white superiors, often referred to as "Tomming" or "signifying" (Gates 50); however, seeing Coleman in this role produces in Tanner the uncomfortable sense that he is looking at a version of himself. Since Coleman is black, the image appears as a negative of his white (or yellow) self, but the identification is undeniable. For Tanner, this is the beginning of a revelation that he sees, at this point, only through a glass darkly. It will take thirty years of companionship with Coleman, a move to New York City, and an encounter with a violent black man for the vision to become clear.

Tanner's response to this discomfiting vision of kinship is to challenge and deny its reality. He engages in dialogue with Coleman designed to assert his white superiority and invoke the racialized social code of the South:

"What you see through those glasses?"
"See a man."

"What kind of man?"
"See the man make theseyer glasses."

"Is he white or black?"
"He white!" the Negro said as if only at that moment was his vision sufficiently improved to detect it. "Yessuh, he white!" he said.
"Well, you treat him like he was white," Tanner said. (CS 539)

O'Connor's handling of the dialogue here is subtly suggestive. Though Coleman finally agrees to abide by the code and recognize Tanner's whiteness, it's clear that he sees Tanner as a man first, *who* he is, rather than *what* he is, a white man. This moment of insight corresponds to Tanner's earlier moment of vision, seeing the humanity of Coleman, *who* he is, a shadow version of himself, instead of seeing *what* he is, a black man. It is significant that Tanner commands Coleman to "treat him like he was white"—as if his whiteness were not existential fact but a matter in question. Henceforward, the men agree to accept the social construction of whiteness, to abide by the performative expectations of the elaborate black/white pantomime, despite the visions they have been given, even though at some level both recognize that it is not grounded in any kind of truth.

For the next thirty years, Tanner and Coleman live this illusion, but their actions reveal a relationship that is very different from the one they pretend to. When Tanner's daughter comes to visit her father, before the fateful move up North, she is shocked to find him living in the same house—a shack the two men built together—with Coleman. Unlike Old Dudley and Rabie, who occupied different floors, Tanner and Coleman sleep in the same room. Granted, Coleman sleeps in a pallet at the foot of Tanner's bed, but as in the conversation the two men first engaged in, we see this as another one of Tanner's attempts to observe the terms of the conventional black/white relationship and deny the obvious kinship the two men share.

Throughout the story, Tanner is defined by his racial pride and, as a white man, defines himself in opposition to blacks. In fact, it is this racial pride that motivates him to make the disastrous decision to leave the

South to move in with his daughter and that proves the root of his undoing. When a black landlord, a local dentist and entrepreneur who goes by the name of Dr. Foley, buys the land he and Coleman squat on, Tanner is appalled to discover that the only condition under which he can stay would be to work for him. O'Connor continues the trope of the race continuum here by characterizing Foley as "only part black. The rest was Indian and white" (*CS* 355), further blurring the lines of distinction Tanner wants to live by. Rather than become subservient to even a half-black man and become "a nigger's white nigger" (a term of Tanner's invention that further suggests the social construction of blackness), the yellow-faced Tanner asserts his whiteness and leaves, only to find himself navigating a world wherein the meaning of race, whiteness, and blackness are all blurred and uncertain, confounding to his southern sensibility, and, finally, deeply mysterious (*CS* 540). By the conclusion of the story, Tanner finally comes to a realization of his pride and the flimsy illusion it was based in, and, as in most O'Connor stories, this revelation arrives through the agency of a catalyst, in this case, the black actor he meets on the stairs of his daughter's apartment building.

Tanner's homesickness manifests itself most powerfully in his loneliness for his black self, Coleman. Thus, it is at first a shock but then a delight for him to discover that a black man has moved into his daughter's building. Though he knows there can never be a substitute for Coleman, he assumes (according to the southern dispensation) he will be able to strike up an unequal friendship with his new neighbor, "handle" him as readily as he was able to "handle" black men in the South, and find some kinship in the alien and unwelcoming place that is New York. Tanner, of course, is sorely mistaken. He encounters the man three times in the hallway and on the stairs, becomes bolder with each meeting in his efforts to communicate, and is rebuffed with increasing severity. The brusque body language of the African American man and his girlfriend and their clear desire to maintain their privacy and avoid any contact are all lost on Tanner, who cannot comprehend a black man's not acceding to the friendly overtures of a white man. Their seemingly destined encounter turns violent when Tanner addresses the man as "Preacher," a term of friendly address used by whites toward blacks in the South (part of the code of manners Tanner knows), but one that carries with it a subtext of condescension. Motivated by "some unfathomable dead-cold rage" (*CS* 544), the black man denies the term of address that would diminish and pigeonhole him, declares his identity as a New Yorker and an actor, and tells Tanner in no uncertain terms that he is an atheist, as far from a preacher as he can get: "I don't believe in that crap. There ain't no Jesus and there ain't no God." In O'Connor's world, as well as Tanner's, these are fighting words, and Tanner responds accordingly: "And you ain't black... and I ain't white!" (CS 545). There is no universe imaginable without Jesus and God any more than there is one imaginable without the foundational human relationship of race. The black actor's vision of reality challenges the very basis of Tanner's universe. Tanner uses irony, of course, to counter the heresy spoken by the actor, but in the world of the story, the words take on an unironic meaning as well, and he speaks a truth he doesn't mean to. In the face of the ultimate, when one stands before the judgment seat of God (an image and eventuality that preoccupies Tanner throughout the story), black and white have no meaning. Human beings are essentially *who* they are, not *what* they are, and race becomes irrelevant. O'Connor has implicitly critiqued race from a social perspective throughout the story, and she now critiques it from a theological perspective as well. Tanner's reward for his inadvertent truth-telling is violence. The actor slams him against the wall, likely inducing a stroke in the old man, and sends him back to his daughter's apartment to lick his wounds.

As he recovers from his stroke, Tanner realizes how necessary it is for him to return home. His daughter has vowed not to bury him in his native southern soil, a betrayal that looms large as he approaches death, and he recognizes Coleman as the only creature on earth he can rely upon to fulfill his last wishes. In his final, heroic effort to escape the confines of the cursed apartment and get home on his own (a delusional venture), Tanner meets his nemesis one last time. Having tumbled down the stairs and asked the actor, who happens to be passing by, for help, the actor's deep-seated rage, likely motivated by a lifetime of racist treatment at the hands of white people, is once more aroused. He misapprehends the white man's addressing him as "Coleman," hearing a racist epithet rather than a term of endearment, "coal man" (CS 549). Confounded and confused, and likely dying, having failed to communicate, Tanner falls back on his earlier form of address, "Preacher," provoking the actor to vent his frustration with the recalcitrant old man once and for all:

> His daughter found him when she came in from the grocery store. His hat had been pulled down over his face and his head and arms thrust between the spokes of the banister; his feet dangled over the stairwell like those of a man in the stocks. She tugged at him frantically and then flew for the police. They cut him out with a saw and said he had been dead an hour. (CS 549)

The sight of old Tanner jammed between the spokes of the banister casts him as a grimly comic figure. The vision of shared "clownishness and captivity" he glimpsed upon first meeting Coleman has at last come to pass and indeed has been the condition of his whole life—something Coleman could see, with his makeshift spectacles, but Tanner could not. Like a man held captive in the stocks and exposed to public ridicule, Tanner pays the price for a lifetime of racial pride and social violence toward African Americans. He dies at the hand of righteous black rage, though he seems only dimly aware of it, believing that he is on his way "home." His broken body is finally cut out with a saw, reminiscent of the sawmill where he once worked, lorded his whiteness over the black men who worked beneath him, and first encountered Coleman.

Coleman clearly functions as Tanner's alter ego, the man who would help him to become a fuller version of himself, and the nameless black actor serves a similar purpose, albeit unwittingly. As is typical of her African American characters, his interior thoughts and identity remain a mystery, but O'Connor provides clues in her descriptions and in the narrative to suggest the motives behind his violent behavior. In his essay "The Black Outsider in O'Connor's Fiction," D. Dean Shackleford sees the actor, with his "horn-rimmed spectacles" and "small almost invisible goatee" as a sinister character whose physical description suggests a demonic or satanic identity (86–87). Shackleford likens the role of the actor to that of another O'Connor character, the large black woman who boards the bus and ultimately strikes Julian's mother in "Everything That Rises Must Converge," another angry African American who refuses to put up with white condescension. O'Connor is similarly reticent, in that story, about the origins of the woman's anger, and in both cases the punishment meted out to the white character, offensive as it may be, seems grossly out of proportion to the crime. Though we recognize the flaws of the racist protagonists, such is the level of violence that our sympathies are expected to lie with them rather than with their attackers. In a sudden and disastrous reversal of roles, white people become the victims and black people the victimizers. Whether this is justice or injustice—or both—is not clear. Again, we are back to the O'Connor's ambivalence regarding the race question and the question of her racial (in)sensitivity.

O'Connor was able to see evidence on a daily basis of the anger of black Americans as the events of the civil rights movement unfolded, anger that she could perceive only from the outside. As a white person who lived in a largely white world, she would have been unable to appreciate firsthand the source of that rage, the privations and challenges to human dignity black people in the South experienced. Her whiteness prevents her from being able to understand black rage and, more to the point, to depict it in a sympathetic way. But, again, O'Connor is aware of her limitations and, instead of pretending to knowledge she lacks, she does what she can to imply possible motivations of these characters. Rather than depicting the African American actor as a devil, as Shackleford suggests, she depicts him as a person blinded by his own inability to see whites as anything other than purveyors of hatred and oppression. His horn-rimmed glasses, rather than a sinister sign, are a correlative to Coleman's glasses—the glasses that enabled him to see Tanner fully and clearly for what he was— only in this case, the glasses ironically prevent the actor from seeing and understanding Tanner and his intentions. Rage can blind a person, and the actor cannot really see who or what is in front of him. All he sees is a white person whom he cannot abide and who, at some level, threatens him. The descriptions of his reactions to Tanner suggest, as Doreen Fowler points out, that the white man provokes terror in him as well as rage ("Writing and Rewriting Race" 34–35). Earlier in the story, he runs from Tanner "as if a swarm of bees had suddenly come down on him out of nowhere," and in a remarkable description of his involuntary physical response to Tanner, a tremor racks him "from his head to his crotch" (*CS* 545), suggesting a fear of emasculation and alluding, perhaps, to the horrible history of castration whites perpetrated on blacks as part of the ritual of lynching. Though O'Connor may not portray the actor sympathetically, she provides signs that Tanner's presence pains him in ways Tanner—who, like his creator, is also blinded by whiteness—can never know. Thus, the story depicts the collision of two men, black and white, who are equally blind to one another, and tragedy inevitably ensues.

And yet, as is typical of O'Connor, the story is a comedy, as well. Through his violence, the actor has inadvertently aided Tanner is his quest to return home. "Home," of course, is the town of Corinth, where Tanner's body will eventually end up, and "home," of course, is God. For all of his failings (and they are many), Tanner is a Christian who has lived his life with the knowledge that he will one day be judged by the God he believes in. There is a clear sense at the end of the story that he will receive a more merciful judgment in heaven than he has on earth. His comic dream of arriving in Georgia in a pine box, being claimed by Coleman and the stationmaster, and springing forth from his coffin like Lazarus from the tomb, shouting "Judgement Day! Judgement Day! Don't you two fools know it's Judgement Day?" (*CS* 546) serves as prediction and prophecy. Tanner knows that going home is the equivalent of resurrection, foolish as his vision of that resurrection may seem. As Richard Giannone observes, "Comic dream speaks to eschatological vision, for folly is one way of reaching the Omega" (243). Tanner has endured a kind of *via crucis* and process of atonement in the form of his northern sojourn. If Tanner had never left the South, he might never have recognized the true nature of his kinship with Coleman, his existential need for his shadow self in order to be whole, and he would have died harboring the delusion that race dictates a human being's worth. His love for Coleman finally outstrips his love for his daughter, his love for his homeland, and his love for himself. Thus, Tanner is saved—twice. And both of his saviors are black.

## "Whiteness Visible"

The experience of T. C. Tanner brings him—and O'Connor's readers—to the realization that there are more dimensions to whiteness than we might have imagined. Like Baby Suggs in Toni Morrison's *Beloved*, O'Connor's story invites us to "ponder color" (4), to consider the many shades that lie between black and white, and to question the color line that Du Bois gave a name to and that has defined (and continues to define) the lives of African Americans. As Valerie Babb demonstrates in her study *Whiteness Visible: The Meaning of Whiteness in American Literature and Culture*—from which the title of this chapter is borrowed—"Whiteness is more than an appearance; it is a system of privileges accorded those with white skin.... As such, whiteness is not a term describing immutable biological content, but rather a term reflecting mutable relationships of social power" (9, 13). Babb does not include O'Connor's fiction in her examination of works by American writers who interrogate the concepts of whiteness and race, but she may well have. The twin visions given to Tanner and Coleman when the latter dons the wooden spectacles open their eyes, if only fleetingly, to the relative nature of race, the accidental (as opposed to essential) meanings ascribed to whiteness and blackness, and to the reality that both are fictive cultural constructions.

That O'Connor accomplishes this without benefit of entering into the minds of her black characters is remarkable. She has, as Alice Walker indicates, granted Rabie, Lutish, Coleman, and the unnamed black men in the New York stairwell their own private thoughts and lives, the freedom to act without explanation and to evade thereby the judgment of readers, black and white. Though O'Connor might have been double-minded about the political solutions to the problem of race in her own time and culture, she might have been limited in her sympathy with African Americans and in her ability to see the world from their perspective, and she might have been selective in her portrayal of the unsavory aspects of the southern racial code people lived by, her dogged attention to "The Geranium" and "Judgement Day" demonstrates her urgent need to create a narrative that does justice to the complexity of the phenomena of race, racial relationship, and racism. It is somehow fitting that "Judgement Day" should be her final story. O'Connor spent her last days and hours of consciousness wrestling with the seemingly intractable problems of race, and then, like the fiercely determined, flawed but faithful Tanner, went home.

## 2 / Race, Politics, and the Double Mind: Flannery's Correspondence versus O'Connor's Fiction

Flannery O'Connor's ideas about race as expressed and embodied in her stories and letters have their origins in multiple sources, as I suggested in the previous chapter. Among those sources are the political events that were unfolding in the South—and across the nation—during the tumultuous years of the civil rights movement. A closer examination of her complex relationship to those events and the varying and even contradictory ways in which she responded to them in her writing provides a helpful framework for understanding O'Connor's fraught perceptions of race, African Americans, and the relationships between blacks and whites.

In her deeply informed and informative essay "The Pivotal Year, 1963: Flannery O'Connor and the Civil Rights Movement," Margaret Early Whitt addresses the strange silence on the part of O'Connor with regard to the "events that were clearly changing the face of the South she knew so well" (79) both in her correspondence and her stories. Focusing on the year 1963, in particular, Whitt chronicles the headline-making events that shocked Americans at their breakfast tables and kept them glued to their televisions as they watched footage of African Americans being sprayed with high-pressure fire hoses and attacked by police dogs in Birmingham, of President Kennedy delivering civil rights talks to the nation, of the news of the assassination of civil rights activist Medgar Evers, and of the March on Washington led by Martin Luther King Jr. and attended by a quarter of a million people (90). O'Connor was a faithful reader of the *Atlanta Constitution* and *The Atlanta Journal*, both of which carried front-page headlines and printed photos capturing most of these events, particularly those that took place in Birmingham in May of that year. By this time

O'Connor and her mother owned a television set as well, acquired in 1961 as a thank-you gift from the Dominican nuns for O'Connor's work on *A Memoir of Mary Ann*, and they would have likely been able to watch the coverage (depending upon their reception) on the news. As Whitt notes, "There were few places on the planet anyone could go and not know about Birmingham" (94).

In the letters O'Connor wrote that year that are readily available to readers (fifty-seven of them published in *Habit of Being* and one in *Collected Works*), she chronicles local happenings, visits from friends, and places she is planning to travel to in order to give lectures. There is only one mention of Birmingham in a letter written in April wherein she reports declining an invitation to offer a presentation at an arts festival in that city (*HB* 514). She makes another brief reference to civil rights–related events in another letter wherein she tells a story that amused her of some "local Negroes" who were planning to integrate the Milledgeville Library only to be thwarted in their efforts by the discovery that it had already been integrated: "That's the way things have to be done here—completely without publicity. Then there is no trouble" (*HB* 542). (As Michael Schroeder points out in his essay "Desegregation and the Silent Character in 'Everything That Rises Must Converge,'" this is the way O'Connor believed change ought to be pursued, "quietly and persistently, and most of all with manners" [77].)

In addition, there are two letters in which she critiques Eudora Welty's remarkable story published in the *New Yorker* in the summer of 1963 in response to the murder of Medgar Evers, "Where Is the Voice Coming From?" The story is a dramatic monologue in which Welty imagines and channels the voice and consciousness of Evers's killer (who had not yet been caught or arrested), vividly portraying the virulent racial hatred she knew so well having lived with it in Mississippi her entire life. (Welty lived only a few blocks from Evers's house, where the murder took place, and was horrified by the near certainty that one of her own neighbors had likely killed him.) O'Connor's first response to the story on August 13 is to admire it: "Nobody else could have got away with it or made it work but her I think. I want to read it again" (*HB* 533). A second response, however, written a few weeks later, offers a very different assessment: "It's the kind of story that the more you think about it the less satisfactory it gets. What I hate most is its being in the *New Yorker* and all the stupid Yankee liberals smacking their lips over typical life in the dear old dirty Southland" (*HB* 537). O'Connor's strong distaste for the story, suggested by the surprising use of the word "hate" to describe a piece she previously admired, is owing in large part to Welty's violation of tribal rules. The fact of a fellow southerner airing the laundry of "the dear old dirty Southland" is bad enough, but publicizing it in a magazine read primarily by northern liberal intellectuals, many of whom hold deeply engrained prejudices about the South, rankles O'Connor. Welty's indignation may be righteous, and her story may reflect truth about the South, but playing into the stereotypes of outsiders incapable of understanding the complexity of southern culture constitutes a form of betrayal, in O'Connor's view. Northern liberals already consider themselves superior, and honest and visceral writing by southerners critiquing the South's social and political problems might readily be misapprehended and (mis)used to confirm their prejudices. Given this perspective, it ought not be surprising that O'Connor concludes the previous comment with the literary pronouncement, mentioned in Chapter 1, "The topical is poison."

Among the few other references to contemporary political and social events, O'Connor makes two brief mentions of the death of President Kennedy, whom she supported, in November 1963 (*HB* 549, 550), and one facetious comment about the March on Washington in a letter to her friend Maryat Lee, in which she offers feigned commiseration with her for her inability to participate in the march due to illness (*HB* 538). Finally, in a wry comment to friend and fellow writer Richard Stern made in a letter in July 1963, she makes brief reference to the racial unrest taking place outside the South: "All us niggers and white folks over here are getting along grand—at least in Georgia and Mississippi. I hear things are not so good in Chicago and Brooklyn but you wouldn't expect them to know what to do with theirself there" (*HB* 532). O'Connor clearly enjoys reminding Stern, who is a displaced southerner, that racial injustice and the call to correct it is not confined to the South and that northerners are no better at solving the difficult problem of race relations than southerners are.

The relative reticence in O'Connor's published letters, as well as her detachment from these disruptive events, puzzles and troubles Whitt, as it has many readers. One might expect O'Connor, "in light of her absolute Christian beliefs and the moral lifestyle to which she was committed," to stand up for justice in some way (81). Whitt goes so far as to invoke Saint Thomas Aquinas, O'Connor's favorite theologian, whose *Summa* she read from each night as *lectio divina* and prelude to her evening prayer, and she accuses O'Connor of committing a sin of omission, albeit of the venial classification, in not making the choice to use her talent as a fiction writer in the service of racial justice. Yet she also reminds the reader that O'Connor "lived her life on one side of a parallel universe—in the white world, not in the black," as did so many white people in the South, most of whom "made a similar non-choice and kept their silences" (81). While this may be true, one might expect writers, people with access to and a deep knowledge of the power of the word, to choose otherwise.

Comparison to Eudora Welty's response to these same events is inevitable. Welty wrote her story "overnight" and in a "straight fury" (Clerc 389, 400), portraying Evers's killer as a paranoid, self-righteous coward who shoots a man in the back in his own driveway because he is tired of seeing Evers's "black nigger face" on television (Welty 727). The story also indicts the governor of Mississippi, Ross Barnett, whose resistance to integration and blatant disregard for the rule of law is interpreted by the murderer as license to kill, though he avers that he did the deed not for any "pat on the back" but for his own "pure-D satisfaction" (Welty 728).

Other white southern writers besides Welty similarly felt righteous rage and the sting of the suffering and injustice experienced by African Americans. Among these is Walker Percy, who laments in *Signposts in a Strange Land*, "The failure of the Christian in the South has been both calamitous and unremarkable. And perhaps this is the worst of it: that no one finds it remarkable" (326). In an essay he wrote for the Catholic magazine *Commonweal* in July 1956 (a year after *Brown vs. Board of Education II* ordered the desegregation of schools "with all deliberate speed"), Percy addresses the problem of the southern Christian's racism and resistance to integration as the result of the South's adherence to the Greek Stoic model of civilization rather than a Judeo-Christian one: "The greatness of the South, like the greatness of the English squirearchy, had always a stronger Greek flavor than it ever had a Christian. Its nobility and graciousness was the nobility and graciousness of the old Stoa" ("Stoicism in the South" 343). In this hierarchical social structure, the upper-class white southerner demonstrated his "generosity toward his fellowmen and above all to his inferiors—not because they were made in the image of God and were therefore lovable in themselves, but because to do them an injustice would be to defile the inner fortress which was oneself" (343). Upper-class whites practiced noblesse oblige toward blacks, enabling the two groups to form an unlikely alliance (in contrast to the conflict between poor whites and blacks), with upper-class whites sympathetic to the cause of justice so long as it was pursued slowly, by degrees, and with manners. The civil rights movement changed all of that: the sight of "the Negro's demanding his rights instead of being thankful for the squire's generosity" (344) is deemed insolence, and the upper-class white southerner, as a result, "is their champion no longer" (342). Percy castigates southern white Christians, including his fellow Catholics (a group that might theoretically include O'Connor), acknowledging the sad fact that instead of defying racism and its attendant injustices, they "have absorbed the local prejudices of the community" (344).

Whitt's essay, along with Welty's story and Percy's remarks, provide a good starting point for an exploration of the relationship between the sweeping public events taking place in the South, the ideas expressed in O'Connor's private correspondence, and the fiction O'Connor is writing—not only in 1963, but throughout the years of unrest she lived through, from 1954, wherein the civil rights era was ignited by the *Brown vs. Board of Education* ruling against segregation, to her death in 1964 just a few weeks before the passing of the Civil Rights Act.

### Early Depictions of Race: "The Barber," "The Geranium," "Wildcat," and "The Coat"

O'Connor's resistance to integration and the civil rights movement has been well established by her biographers and critics, mostly on the basis of her correspondence. However, it has also been noted that O'Connor had been more sympathetic to the political and social plight of African Americans earlier in her life. Brad Gooch sums up O'Connor's shift in sentiment in his biography, *Flannery*, saying that her "position had shifted from the shocking contrariness of the girl who wrote from the point of view of black characters in her high school stories and decried the segregated buses she rode to Atlanta as a graduate student, to one of complex ambivalence. She had returned to settle in a society predicated on segregation and had taken on its charged voices and manners as the setting of her fiction" (332). Gooch here refers to an incident O'Connor recounts in one of her letters to her friend Elizabeth Hester, written November 16, 1957, wherein she reports overhearing a bus driver's rude remark to the African Americans riding his bus, referring to them as "stovepipe blondes" and urging them to "git in the back." O'Connor states, at that "moment I became an integrationist" (*HB* 253). During this same period as the bus incident, O'Connor had struck up a friendship with an African American graduate student, Gloria Bremerwell, when she was pursuing her MFA at Iowa. When warned by her mother that interracial relationships were dangerous, O'Connor replied that she would not allow her friendships to be constrained by matters of race (Wood, *Christ-Haunted South* 102).

In addition to this evidence of more progressive political leanings in her letters, the stories O'Connor was writing as a graduate student bespeak an interest in and a consciousness of the complexities of the race question. During her time at Iowa (1945–48), a new barbershop opened up in town with the express intention of accommodating black students who were unable to get haircuts from the so-called "Jim Crow barbers" in town or on campus. This became a controversial issue locally and a subject of conversation in the Workshop, since one of the members, African American student Herb Nipson, had formerly needed to travel twenty-one miles for a haircut (Gooch 131). The result of these events and conversations is O'Connor's story, "The Barber," written in 1946 as part of her master's thesis, in which she explores the racial dynamics of her own culture by relocating the barber shop in the South. Though the story is apprentice work, it adumbrates some of the elements with regard to the treatment of white and black characters that will become evident in her mature work. The story's protagonist is a college professor named Rayber, the archetypal man of liberal thought and politics who will later reappear in various incarnations in O'Connor's fiction: as Julian in "Everything That Rises Must Converge," Asbury in "The Enduring Chill," Sheppard in "The Lame Shall Enter First," and Rayber in *The Violent Bear It Away*. Rayber has voted for the progressive candidate in the white Democratic primary and is accused by his barber of being "a nigger-lover." Taken off guard by the scathing language of the barber, who has cast his vote for Hawkson, the conservative candidate who has vowed to "put these niggers in their places," Rayber is stunned into silence, though afterward he wishes he had offered the dignified and measured response, "I am neither a Negro- or a white-lover" (CS 16, 15). This establishes the pattern of the story, wherein Rayber is repeatedly subject to the barber's racist rants and is incapable of formulating an intellectually grounded resistance to his corrupt ideas. Not only is the ugly face of southern bigotry put on display, but so too is the ineffectual posturing of the white liberal. Despite all of his education, Rayber cannot argue effectively with the barber because he does not know what he believes. Rayber finally writes out a rebuttal, after sweating over it all day, but then botches his delivery so badly he leaves the barber and his crew of regulars in a state of confused silence immediately interrupted by laughter. Rayber's final response to this humiliation is wordless rage. He punches the barber in the face and runs from the shop, his face half-lathered, the barber's bib "dangling to his knees" (CS 25).

O'Connor's satire on the white liberal enterprise is clear. Rayber, who suffers from intellectual pride, is reduced to a petulant child (as suggested by the barber's bib). His double-mindedness about race is also betrayed in more subtle ways. In her essay "Aligning the Psychological with the Theological: Doubling and Race in Flannery O'Connor's Fiction," Doreen Fowler notes that Rayber is always measuring himself against his colleague, a philosophy professor named Jacobs, whom he wants to engage in debate on the question of race. Jacobs, who is not a liberal despite all of his education, puzzles Rayber, and yet Rayber holds him up as a sort of model, wondering as he is crafting his response to the barber "how Jacobs would have done it" as "Jacobs had a way about him of making people think he knew more than Rayber thought he knew" (*CS* 22). Perhaps what he finds compelling about Jacobs is his honesty about his racism: "He remembers Jacobs telling him about lecturing at a Negro college for a week. They couldn't say Negro—nigger—colored—black. Jacobs said he had come home every night and shouted, 'NIGGER NIGGER NIGGER' out the back window" (*CS* 16). As Fowler argues, Jacobs's enforced repression of his racism at the Negro college is a version of Rayber's repression of his own racist ideology, only Jacobs is at least aware of his while Rayber is completely lacking in this critical self-knowledge ("Aligning the Psychological with the Theological" 84). Such an insight is telling. The young O'Connor knows repressed racism from her own experience as a white person growing up in the racist South, having heard such racist talk all her life and having inevitably endured her own lapses in charity toward her black brothers and sisters—a knowledge that positions her well to dramatize the forms it takes in her white characters. It also affords her the opportunity to ridicule the pathetic efforts made by white liberals to render themselves color blind and shows O'Connor critiquing the concept.

This critique is prescient on O'Connor's part. There was a time when color blindness was thought to be conducive to better race relations in American society: experience has proven, however, that this denial of obvious difference between human beings is impossible and produces undesirable effects, as Jacobs's experience demonstrates. Well-intentioned as it may have been in its inception, the concept has been discredited as a means and method of redressing racial injustice. According to Terrance MacMullan, whose work on the philosophy of whiteness elucidates a number of misapprehensions about race awareness, color blindness constitutes "a facile response to racism in practice." MacMullan goes on to observe that "Whiteness has so thoroughly permeated our perspectives, habits and institutions that it is unrealistic to think that we can quickly go from centuries of legalized white supremacism . . . to race-blind fairness" ("Facing Up to Ignorance and Privilege" 650). As MacMullan suggests in his essay, white people have little sense of themselves as racialized human beings, but they very clearly perceive color differences between black people and themselves. This perception is accompanied by racial stereotypes and prejudices white people may or may not be conscious of. American society is largely built on these unspoken prejudicial assumptions, and they exercise a powerful influence on our social institutions and interactions, including our customs with regard to marriage, property ownership, and hiring practices. For white people to try to pretend that they do not perceive race differences and do not harbor the prejudices that go with them would be delusional. In addition, because they are mostly blind to the ways in which racial inequality has shaped society, they would not see the need to dismantle and reform its racist institutions, nor would they know how to go about doing it even if they perceived the need. In fact, most white Americans, if asked, would likely claim to be color-blind, a misapprehension that demonstrates a blindness to everything but race. There is something fundamentally dishonest, as well as ineffectual, about the concept of color blindness. Along similar lines, race scholars Richard Delgado and Jean Stefanic argue that color blindness allows us to ameliorate "only the extremely egregious racial harms, ones that everyone would notice and condemn. But if racism is embedded in our thought processes and social structures ... then the 'ordinary business' of society ... will keep minorities in subordinate positions. Only aggressive, color-conscious efforts to change the way things are will do much to ameliorate misery" (27).

Though the introduction of race-blind practice might help to correct situations where blatant racism is at work, it would not help in situations where racism is subtle, implicit, and, therefore, more insidious. Looking directly at race and acknowledging racial difference as a reality of life helps the members of a culture to be conscious of race as a social construction, to perceive the ways in which the concept has shaped society, and to develop strategies to correct injustice. In her characterization of Rayber and Jacobs and her pairing of them as foils, O'Connor demonstrates herself to be well ahead of her time as she puzzles out the complexities and inconsistencies she observes in the racial attitudes and behaviors in the people around her.

Finally, O'Connor demonstrates another kind of racial savvy in her characterization of George, the black man who works in the barbershop. Throughout his ordeal, Rayber is aware of George's presence and wonders what his politics might be. Yet, for all of his supposed high-mindedness with regard to racial equality, Rayber thinks of George as the barber's "boy." The narrator, who channels Rayber's consciousness, uses this racially demeaning term consistently, even though George is clearly old enough to vote, thus betraying Rayber's ignorance of his own racism. O'Connor, as is typical of her in her later writing, never tries to enter George's consciousness. Instead, she sticks to what she knows and portrays the skillful ways in which African Americans navigate the racial minefield of daily life. When asked by the barber whom he will vote for, George responds cagily, providing the only answer that would be acceptable to his white boss and pledging his vote for the conservative racist candidate: "I don't know is they gonna let me vote.... Do, I gonna vote for Mr. Hawkson" (*CS* 25). The white men, of course, are equally aware of this code, or "cabala," as James Baldwin calls it ("They Can't Turn Back" 622), as a fiction they all live by. When Rayber demands that the code be broken by having the barber call George from the back so he can listen to Rayber's speech as a man among equals, the barber responds knowingly: "He can hear back where he is.... He can hear what he hears and he can hear two times that much. He can hear what you don't say as well as what you do" (*CS* 24). The barber justifies the racist code, without which none of the people present, white or black, know how to function, but he also credits George with a kind of critical judgment that is lacking in Rayber. In addition, he indicts Rayber as a closet racist, a charge substantiated by Rayber's interior thoughts. A further instance of this in the story occurs when Rayber is looking out the window of the barber shop and thinks he sees Jacobs walking across the square when his vision is blocked by "three colored boys in zoot suits" who stop in front of the shop and lean against the window "making a hole in the view" (*CS* 20). The black men (called "boys" in Rayber's mind) get in the way of Rayber's ability to see what truly matters to him, his white colleague. African Americans are a nuisance to Rayber, their dark skin creating a "hole" in his vision, rendering him blind. For him, "the Negro" constitutes vacuous space rather than substance. This is not lost on the barber or on George. In Fowler's words, "George can hear that what is missing from Rayber's verbal posturing is any identification with African Americans. Rayber's speech is characterized by what he doesn't say, by a repression of any recognition of a shared humanity with people whose subjection supports a privileged white identity" ("Aligning the Psychological with the Theological" 85). Rayber's liberalism is pure posturing, and, ironically, his treatment of George is less respectful than the frankly racist barber's.

For all of her critical insight into the weaknesses of liberal politics, as evidenced in the story, O'Connor clearly identified with liberalism more closely than she did the openly racist politics of her fellow southerners. As is ever the case, it takes one to know one—though the same might be said for her accurate portrayal of white racist politics. Thus, "The Barber" is an expression of her own double-mindedness with regard to matters of race and politics—an ambivalence that will continue to grow and manifest itself in her later stories, most visibly in her story showcasing another hapless shallow liberal, Julian, and his conservative mother, "Everything That Rises Must Converge."

In assessing O'Connor's stories written during her time at Iowa, it becomes clear that she is experimenting, trying to figure out how to write about race, or, at least, how to portray it faithfully in her fiction. This experimentation is also evident in "The Geranium" (as discussed at some length in Chapter 1). In contrast to "The Barber," we recognize it as a story that is fully sympathetic to northern liberal politics, and, in fact more so than any she would write in the course of her career. The old racist dispensation of white superiority and black subordination, represented by Old Dudley's paternalistic relationship to his "negro" sidekick, Rabie, is displaced by a new relationship between whites and blacks, as represented by the conversation between the black man Dudley meets in the hallway of his daughter's apartment building. "While Dudley is predictably vicious in his racist attitudes, his black counterpart is predictably virtuous in his patience and charity," observes Ralph Wood in his analysis of the story ("Where Is the Voice Coming From?" 99). His condescension toward Dudley demonstrates that this is not even a conversation between equals but a clear reversal of the traditional roles played by whites and blacks in the South, wherein the young black man treats the old white man like an aged child, infantilizing and emasculating him as Dudley once infantilized and emasculated Rabie. There is a simplicity to the characterization of both Dudley and his black neighbor here, lending the story a schematic effect. This is something she would later correct and complicate in "Judgement Day." But the story, and particularly the portrayal of the black man as a smart, savvy, independent adult, is a new departure for her.

In addition to "The Geranium" and "The Barber," it is worth noting that during this period O'Connor wrote the only two stories of her career in which she adopts the point of view of an African American protagonist, "Wildcat" and "The Coat." The former story was one of the seven she eventually submitted as her master's thesis, whereas the latter was unpublished and unknown until 1996 when it was discovered by Sally Fitzgerald and published in *DoubleTake* magazine. As is the case with most juvenilia, neither story shows O'Connor at her best, but both testify to her conscious effort to enlarge her sensibility and contain suggestions of the writer she will become. "Wildcat" portrays the terror of Old Gabriel, an aged blind black man who waits for what he believes is his imminent death in the form of a wildcat that prowls the woods outside his cabin. According to Sarah Gordon, "There are no attacks on cultural foolishness and pretentiousness, no vivid descriptions, and no satirical narrative voice: instead, O'Connor tells this story about a black community through old Gabriel's consciousness and in a dialect so clumsy the narrative nearly breaks with the strain" (68). Gordon's assessment of the story as unequal to O'Connor's mature work is accurate, though O'Connor's supposedly clumsy rendering of dialect is overstated. In fact, the attempt to write the story in dialect—particularly the long interior monologue that dramatizes Gabriel's blind terror—shows O'Connor teaching herself how to handle idiom, a technique she will master in her later stories. It is also clear that she is making a valiant attempt to gain access to a mind and a culture that is very different from her own. Young O'Connor, having grown up in a segregated society, had to imagine herself into Gabriel's history, his childhood relationship with his mother, as well as into his present life, living in a houseful of black men and boys (his grandsons) who hunt and cook for themselves and tease each other in a way that, in fact, foreshadows the adult/child relationships shared by characters in her later stories, especially that between Nelson and Mr. Head in "The Artificial Nigger." O'Connor is stretching herself in terms of both race and gender, imagining not only black lives but also men's lives. However, much as the reader is meant to sympathize with the protagonist, we remain detached and Gabriel remains isolated in his terror, even from his grandsons. There is less a sense of pathos than the pathetic in the rendering of the character. O'Connor is more successful in "The Geranium" at making an old man's state of mind accessible to the reader.

"The Coat," on the other hand, is a more engaging tale. Here O'Connor channels the consciousness of an elderly black washerwoman, Rosa, who is married to a stereotypically irresponsible black man given to laziness and drunkenness. Rosa stumbles on the body of a white man in the woods one day, and when her husband comes home drunk and tells the story of having found a coat that he has sold for wine and cash, she begins to fear that he has killed the man. Her husband convinces her of his innocence, but Rosa insists that they bury the body anyway to avoid being accused of murder. While he is burying the corpse, a group of white men happen by, interrogate him, and kill him when he panics. Afterward, as Rosa grieves the death of her husband, she learns that the lost coat belonged to the husband of one of her customers: "He had lost it last week in the woods and found that some colored man had taken ten dollars out the pocket and exchanged the coat at Branches for four pints of cheap wine. Wasn't that ridiculous? She knew Mr. Wilkinson had paid at least twenty dollars for that coat" (41). The white woman has the last words in this story, as white people do in life, but at the heart of the tale is Rosa's consciousness and voice, which the apprentice O'Connor renders with sensitivity and fidelity. The cruel irony of Rosa's fate is affecting, and her identity as a woman afflicted by the injustices of a racist caste system comes through clearly. The young O'Connor effectively presents the world as seen through Rosa's eyes and as heard through Rosa's ears. The protagonist's interior thoughts are rendered sympathetically in dialect (again demonstrating O'Connor's experimentation), showing her to be bright, reflective, and devoted to both her family and her God. Rosa's strength of character, sense of humor, and comic frustration with her errant husband is evident in the dialogue they share, and at the conclusion the reader fully feels the poignancy of the fate of these two hapless people, especially Rosa's. As biographer Jean Cash observes: "In this story, in which she uses a third-person limited perspective, O'Connor is definitely inside the black woman's head" (104). Given the relative success of this early experiment, it seems strange that O'Connor would ultimately assert that she was unable to see from the point of view of black characters.

In her analysis of these early stories, Janet Egleson Dunleavy suggests that O'Connor's doubting of her ability to portray the African American perspective and her failure to make any later attempts "invites reconsideration" and raises some provocative questions:

> Was it because, given the changes that were affecting black/white relations in the 1950s and 1960s, she felt less sure in those years about what Southern blacks were thinking and feeling than in the 1940s when she wrote "The Geranium" . . . and "The Wildcat"? Was it because increasingly during the 1950s and 1960s the credibility of white writers who portrayed blacks in their fiction was being challenged? Or was it because she declined to present as an evocation of the inner consciousness of blacks images she regarded as protective masks? (194)

Dunleavy's first question suggests that as the civil rights era progressed and the formerly private thoughts of African Americans were being publicly expressed, O'Connor may have felt less confident in her understanding of her black neighbors. This theory would imply that O'Connor was experiencing an awakening to the complexity and opacity of black people, whom she had previously seen as relatively simple and transparent. The second question, regarding the perceived credibility of white writers to represent black experience, addresses the idea of authorial limitation, in both O'Connor's own work and that of her contemporaries—a condition O'Connor was surely becoming more aware of as she practiced her craft. It is also worth noting that O'Connor wanted to publish her work and may have feared (justifiably) that stories about black people written by a white southern woman would not appeal to editors, publishers, and, readers. Finally, the third question (which is related to Dunleavy's first question) suggests that O'Connor made a conscious choice not to presume, in her characterization of African Americans, that the face black people show to whites is an accurate reflection of their true selves. O'Connor certainly lived with this reality, in accordance with the southern code of manners that governed interactions between blacks and whites, but perhaps only gradually became conscious of it and began to understand its implications for her fiction.

These possibilities are all worthy of consideration, though in the absence of evidence, one cannot definitively prove or disprove any of them. An additional—and, perhaps less speculative—explanation for O'Connor's decision as a mature artist to avoid this terrain might be traceable to her developing sense of what constitutes cultural appropriation and authorial authenticity. It seems that O'Connor was willing to cross the color line—artistically and imaginatively, as well as physically—while living away at school in Iowa, far from the segregated world of the South. In fact, it is arguable that the color line became visible to her only after she escaped the region and lived in a place where it was not so fully and indisputably present. However, upon her return to the culture she was raised in, she may have felt uncomfortable and perhaps even presumptuous in crossing that line. Once her illness forced her to take up residence in Milledgeville, O'Connor's world became considerably smaller and the gestures one makes within that world became fraught with meanings one was not necessarily in control of. Nearly all of her day-to-day contact would have been with people who rigidly observe the racial code, and the society of racist white people became both her home and the subject for her fiction. Since white people and their folly gave her plenty to write about, she probably saw no need to cross that line.

In the end, as Alice Walker suggests, O'Connor's practice might be seen as a gesture to preserve the dignity of her black characters, and, by extension, the dignity of African Americans, by not claiming knowledge of their mystery. Indeed, O'Connor once stated, "The uneducated Southern Negro is not the clown he's made out to be. He's a man of very elaborate manners and great formality which he uses superbly for his own protection and to insure his own privacy" (Magee 104). O'Connor acknowledges the mask African Americans must wear in order to maintain a sense of autonomy amid a culture with the historical legacy of slavery. Though slave owners could—and did—commit the outrage of claiming ownership of black bodies, they could not possess their minds. Interiority was the one arena of freedom African Americans could lay claim to in the era of slavery, and it continues to be a source of freedom in the Jim Crow era of the South. O'Connor goes on to acknowledge that this circumstance is not desirable but is, nonetheless, necessary: "All this may not be ideal, but the Southerner has enough sense not to ask for the ideal but only for the possible, the workable. The South has survived in the past because its manners, however lopsided or inadequate they may have been, provided enough social discipline to hold us together and give us an identity" (Magee 104). The identity O'Connor lays claim to, both as an artist and as a citizen of the South, is one borne of segregation. Thus, for better or for worse, O'Connor would thereafter hold her black characters at a distance (as discussed in Chapter 1) and dwell in the world of whites.

## Later Thoughts on Race: O'Connor's Correspondence

While it is true that O'Connor's correspondence contains very little commentary on specific events of the civil rights movement, her letters are quite expressive regarding her thoughts and feelings about race. Nowhere is this more evident than in her seven-year correspondence with Maryat Lee. O'Connor and Lee met in December 1956, and despite vast differences in their personalities and politics they became fast friends. Lee, the sister of Dr. Robert E. Lee, president of Flannery's alma mater, Georgia State College for Women in Milledgeville, had been born and bred in the South but moved northward to attend Wellesley College and then to New York City in order to pursue a career as a playwright. O'Connor, too, had lived in New York, and had achieved some literary notoriety by the time she and Lee met at Andalusia; however, the trajectories of their lives were very different. Whereas O'Connor had left behind her literary adventures in the North to return to Georgia (albeit unwillingly) and had readapted herself to the ethos of the South, Lee's education and life in the North had permanently shaped her politics and her views on race. Jean W. Cash in her essay on the friendship shared by O'Connor and Lee describes Maryat as "a pioneering and artistic feminist" who "travelled the streets of Harlem," advocated for the rights of African Americans, and constituted what was for O'Connor, as well as Lee's own family, an anomaly as a southern liberal ("Maryat and Flanneryat" 64). This difference in their outlooks fascinated O'Connor and provided her with the welcome opportunity to dialogue and debate about the important topic of race, along with other issues (especially writing and illness) that mattered to them both.

One of the most telling (and well-known) exchanges between the two friends took place in April 1959, wherein Maryat asks Flannery whether she might invite African American writer and activist James Baldwin to visit her at Andalusia. O'Connor's response is as unequivocal as it is now (in)famous:

> No I can't see James Baldwin in Georgia. It would cause the greatest trouble and disturbance and disunion. In New York it would be nice to meet him: here it would not. I observe the traditions of the society I feed on—it's only fair. Might as well expect a mule to fly as me to see James Baldwin in Georgia. I have read one of his stories and it was a good one. (*HB* 329)

The letter itself embodies O'Connor's contradictory attitude and paradoxical position: both her respect for Baldwin as a writer and her inability to meet with him as a colleague and an equal. The key to her response lies in the different manners and expectations associated with the two very different worlds she has lived in—New York and Georgia. In April 1959 rural Georgia was a place mostly untouched (as yet) by civil rights unrest. Free blacks and whites had been living together for a century, yet they might as well have lived worlds apart, obeying the careful code of "separate but equal," the established norm kept in force through a rigid system of Jim Crow apartheid and through the very real threat of violence from the Ku Klux Klan. As a reminder of this dispensation, in another letter to Maryat Lee, O'Connor describes the events that occurred on the campus of her alma mater in the late 1940s wherein two African American teachers attended an education conference held at the university: "The story goes that everything was as separate and equal as possible, even down to two Coca-Cola machines, white and colored; but that night a cross was burned on Dr. Wells' [the college president's] side lawn. And those times weren't as troubled as these" (*HB* 195). O'Connor concludes this grim tale with a characteristically comic deflation of the Klansmen responsible for these actions: "The people who burned the cross couldn't have gone past the fourth grade but, for the time they were mighty interested in education" (*HB* 195). O'Connor's point is a painful one. Redneck fools that they may be, these men exercise power. For half a century and more, much of the South, both white and black (as well as Catholic and Jew), has lived in thrall to a terrorist organization that makes sure there is no contact between blacks and whites that they judge to be illicit. Given this, it is no wonder O'Connor could not host Baldwin at her home. To do so would not only offend her mother and scandalize her neighbors, it would put them all, Baldwin included, in danger. Seen in this context, her decision to abide by "the traditions of the society she feeds on" seems as much a survival mechanism as a capitulation to racial intolerance.

That said, it is important to note the language O'Connor uses in describing her relationship to the white culture she is living in the midst of. As Carole K. Harris notes in her analysis of this exchange, O'Connor feeds on the people of her town "as source material for her fictional characters, so she does not want to show ingratitude by disrespecting their manners ... yet, at heart she's protecting herself. ... O'Connor is the one who would suffer should she break the code and receive Baldwin as a visitor" (2). O'Connor is, in a sense, living incognito, seeming to be part of the culture yet standing outside of it, observing and critiquing, as writers tend to do. Being a writer is like being a spy in the enemy camp, and the last thing a spy wants is to have her cover blown. This is one possible implication of this rather strange metaphor O'Connor invokes. Another possible interpretation, however, is less savory but no less likely. Biologically speaking, one becomes one, in a sense, with what one feeds on. The relationship implied by O'Connor's image might be seen as akin to that between a host and a parasite. The more the parasite ingests of the host, the more intertwined the two become, to the point where one can't be separated from the other. O'Connor's implication of her own gradual assimilation into the culture suggests she sees herself becoming part and parcel of it—a highly undesirable circumstance for a writer. Finally, as if to seal the difference between the two worlds she and Maryat Lee inhabit, O'Connor invokes a southern figure of speech, "Might as well expect a mule to fly as me to see James Baldwin in Georgia," using local language and color—notably substituting the stubborn mule for the conventional pig—to describe a physical impossibility. O'Connor invokes the authority of southern manners and southern speech in her forceful denial of Maryat's request, the kind only a Yankee liberal (or a disaffected southerner) would make.

O'Connor expresses tolerance and even admiration of the outspoken Baldwin in this letter, despite the well- publicized trips to the South he had been making since 1957 in order to witness and protest the practice of segregation. Five years later, in another letter to Maryat Lee dated May 21, 1964, she expresses a different sentiment:

> About the Negroes, the kind I don't like is the philosophizing prophesying pontificating kind, the James Baldwin kind. Very ignorant but never silent. Baldwin can tell us what it feels like to be a Negro in Harlem but he tries to tell us everything else too. M. L. King I don't think is the ages great saint but he's at least doing what he can do & has to do. Don't know anything about Ossie Davis

except you like him but you probably like them all. My question is usually, would this person be endurable if white. If Baldwin were white nobody would stand him a minute. (*CW* 1208)

O'Connor's dislike for Baldwin, along with her distaste for other outspoken African Americans, is as disturbing as it is frank. She faults Baldwin for speaking about things he doesn't know about, namely the code that seemingly only southerners know and understand, although in his writings it is clear that he grasps the meaning of "the cabala" quite well ("They Can't Turn Back" 622; see discussion in Chapter 1). O'Connor's frustration with Baldwin seems to be as much due to his northern perspective as his black perspective, both of which are partial (she would likely argue) and not based in familiarity and sympathy with the complicated manners of the South. Even so, the language O'Connor uses here is classic racist language—telling Maryat that she probably likes "them all," casting African Americans as a monolithic group that constitutes the Black Other for white people and perpetuating an us-versus-them mentality, and implying resentment at a supposed double standard for blacks and whites that casts blacks (incredibly enough) as the recipients of kinder public treatment. One activist who escapes her harsh judgment (albeit narrowly) is Martin Luther King, whom she allows to play the triple roles of "philosophizing prophesying and pontificating Negro" most likely because he is a southerner who knows whereof he speaks when it comes to segregation and because he is a committed Christian and pastor. O'Connor implicitly acknowledges that his activism is driven by his vocation, "what he has to do" on behalf of his flock and fellow human beings in the face of injustice. Even so, she feels it necessary to mock King and knock him from his pedestal, denying his status as secular saint. This is vintage O'Connor: From her theological vantage point, all human beings are sinners, white and black, and she bristles at hagiography of any kind. It is further worth noting that in this letter O'Connor goes on to express a liking for Cassius Clay, using his Christian rather than his Muslim name, Muhammad Ali, despite the announcement of his name change two months before on March 6, 1964. O'Connor's admiration for Clay/Ali is likely due to his identification with black separatism, a position more in keeping with her own negative views of integration. She clearly enjoys the characteristically flamboyant language he uses in describing the fraught and seemingly irreparable relationship between blacks and whites, quoting his words in a television interview: "If a tiger move into the room with you . . . and you leave, that dont mean you hate the tiger. Just means you know you and him can't make out" (*CW* 1208–09).

She concludes her comments on Clay/Ali lamenting his conversion to Islam, "Cassius is too good for the Moslems," effectively denigrating the faith and the religious community he has adopted and demonstrating a distrust of the Nation of Islam shared by many contemporary Americans (*CW* 1209). Of course, it should be noted that O'Connor was not alone in her critique of black activists. Such criticism was common enough for Baldwin to observe, "The power of the white world is threatened whenever a black man refuses to accept the white world's definitions. So every attempt is made to cut that black man down" (*The Fire Next Time* 69). Ultimately, O'Connor's disdain for African American activists seems to confirm Baldwin's prescient and prophetic assessment.

## "The Habit of Bigotry" and "The Protean N-word"

Given her allergy to hagiography, it is ironic that hagiography of O'Connor herself is at least one motive behind the defensive postures many critics and biographers take regarding her attitudes toward race. There is general, though by no means universal, reluctance to acknowledge or to come to terms with what Paul Elie calls "the habit of bigotry" that imbues her correspondence, especially in the letters exchanged with Maryat Lee. Elie's characterization of the letters, quoted earlier in my introduction, is worth reviewing here: "There is the word 'nigger' running through the correspondence. There are quips about blacks, offered again and again as punch lines. There is, in the letters, a habit of bigotry that grows more pronounced as O'Connor's fiction, in the matters of race, grows more complex and profound—a habit that seems to defy the pattern of her art" (327).

In discussing the events of the civil rights movement and the questions it raised about race, Lee and O'Connor developed a kind of patter in their correspondence, described by biographer Brad Gooch, wherein "Maryat was cast as the ultimate Northern liberal, and Flannery a bigoted Southern redneck. Unfortunately, in a number of these letters, many still unpublished, Flannery slipped into her role too easily, her mask fitting disconcertingly well. She turned out to be a connoisseur of racial jokes, regaling Maryat with offensive punch lines" (335). The two women adopted pet names as part of this game, and, along with them, alternate personalities: Flannery dubbed Maryat "Raybutter," "Raybalm," and "Rayfish"—all variations on Rayber, Maryat's favorite character in *The Violent Bear It Away*—and Maryat invented nicknames for Flannery based on the boy prophet she so identified with, including "Tarbabe," "Tarsoul," "Tarsquawk," and "Tarfunk." It is impossible to know the degree to which

O'Connor's participation in this play was ironic, her jokes told purely for effect in a lame (not to mention insensitive) attempt at humor, and the degree to which she actually believed in the racial inferiority these jokes assumed. But the fact that the jokes are told at all demonstrates at the very least an insensitivity to the suffering of African Americans, past and present, as well as a lack of a sense of responsibility for being, in some ways, an agent and beneficiary of that suffering.

This insensitivity is evident in one such joke that appears in a letter Flannery writes to Maryat on November 17, 1962, after a brief visit to Texas. Although the letter appears in *The Habit of Being* (499), the joke that follows is expurgated: "I also heard a nice Texas joke. Somebody from Texas calls up the White House, says 'Is President Kennedy there?' 'Nawsuh he aint here.' 'Well is Miss Jackie there?' 'She aint here neither.' 'Well where is Mr. Lyndon?' 'He done gone too.' 'Well who's running things up there?' 'We is'" (Emory). Seen on its own, the joke is clearly a piece of political satire designed primarily to critique the Kennedy administration as a puppet government for its support of civil rights. The obvious fiction is that the people who are really pulling the strings are African Americans, not the white people elected to office. The supposed humor turns on the seemingly absurd idea that black people (the "we" of the punch line, spoken in black dialect, bad grammar intact) would be capable of running the government. As is implied by his speech, the image of the person on the other end of the line is that of the stereotypical darkie, servile and foolish, suited to answering phones and acting as a servant at the White House, but certainly not to governing the country. The nightmare scenario is depicted as the disastrous result of the liberal attitude toward race, to the mind of a Texan (or a conservative southerner, for that matter), and it bespeaks the fear of whites of what may eventually come of integration and the drive for equal rights. The fact that O'Connor repeats the joke to Maryat Lee lends it an additional valence. It gives her the opportunity to skewer her friend for her liberal politics (even though O'Connor suffers collateral damage, since she is a Kennedy supporter, despite his civil rights agenda). The accidental darkie president is *her* fault. The telling of the joke also serves as an endorsement of its main message and serves to convey O'Connor's own opinion about the potentially catastrophic end of such politics—the ruination of the country as its destiny falls into the hands of African Americans, a blatantly inferior people.

It is worth noting that O'Connor also shared the joke in a letter to writer Richard Stern who, as was mentioned earlier, was a displaced southerner, like Maryat Lee. (Though the joke remains unpublished in the collected letters, it appears in a brief tribute Stern wrote for *Shenandoah* after O'Connor's death.) A theme common in O'Connor's correspondence with both friends is that the South is a better place for a writer to live and work than Chicago, New York, or Europe—a point she is serious about, tongue-in-cheek though the tone may be. In her letter to Stern, she notes after the joke, "I am trying to make you homesick before your [Fulbright] year is out" (Stern 10). In the context of her correspondence with Stern, the joke takes on a slightly different valence. O'Connor is not playing the role of southern bigot she often played with Maryat Lee. Instead, she comes across as a writer who is proud of her native South, despite the supposedly more sophisticated places one might visit and live: "You are not the only one that's been somewheres. I just got back from Texas" (10). The "nice Texas joke" she tells attests to southern wit and to the South's nuanced understanding of the potential consequences of the civil rights movement. O'Connor's tribalism becomes evident here, as it does in her remarks about Eudora Welty's *New Yorker* story—only here we see two southern writers sharing a moment of quiet collusion.

Gooch's side note that the most egregious of O'Connor's jokes and remarks show up in letters that are, as yet, unpublished also speaks to the theme of hagiography mentioned earlier. In addition, in reading the letters housed in the special collections at Georgia College and State University and Emory University, as mentioned in my Introduction, one discovers that numerous passages have been omitted from the published versions of the letters that appear in *The Habit of Being* and *Collected Works*. The joke quoted above constitutes one such passage. The reluctance of the O'Connor estate to publish these letters and the decision to require excerpting from others speaks to this desire to protect O'Connor's reputation and to let readers see her in the best light, but it is noteworthy that what one finds in the unpublished letters and excerpted passages differs not so much in kind from what is in the published ones, but in degree. For instance, in a letter Flannery writes on May 21, 1962, she makes the facetious suggestion to Maryat that she come to visit Milledgeville and attempt to have some of her trip paid for by the local government:

> I have a plan for you. Come South at your own expense and let the White Citizens Council send you back. You could tell them that you was a little light but a guaranteed nigger. This would cut your expenses in half and give you a nice vacation in the land of sin and guilt. You could even go to Hyannisport. I wish this wasn't for real and then I could have made it up. (*HB* 475)

The objects of O'Connor's keen satire here are multiple—the local racist council, the Kennedys and their northern liberal civil rights agenda, and, of course, the bleeding heart Maryat, whose sympathy with black people is so great she has practically become one. It is a shock, in the midst of this witty sparring, to see Flannery use the crude word "nigger." Although it might be argued that she uses it ironically here, channeling the sensibility of the White Citizens Council, it is unsettling nonetheless. It is even more unsettling to see the full letter as originally written. What has been excised from the published version is the salutation, which reads "Dear Nigger Loving New York White Woman," and the valediction, which reads "Yours Neutral to Niggers" (GCSU). There is a perverse delight in O'Connor's (il)liberal overuse of the word "nigger" here—a deliberate desire to shock the sensibility of her sensitive friend—even as she puts her own insensitivity on display. While it's true that she is implicitly castigating the South for being "the land of guilt and sin," and seemingly claims that sin as her own, her comfortable use of that uncomfortable term suggests that she is reveling in being part of that ethos. In addition, the letter contains a second objectionable epithet as she accuses her friend of being a so-called "nigger-lover," a derogatory term most often applied to whites sympathetic to the civil rights movement, as Maryat was. Meanwhile, Flannery characterizes her own position, in contrast to Maryat's objectionable one (by southern standards), as one of neutrality, implying that it is a saner and less laughable political stance. This, of course, is not how the reader perceives her position. History has proven, again and again, the maxim (attributed to many sources, ranging from Edmund Burke to Abraham Lincoln), "All that is required for evil to prosper is that good men do nothing." O'Connor, consciously or not, casts herself as the Switzerland of the civil rights movement.

There is no doubt that Americans living in the early part of the twenty-first century are sensitized to the word "nigger" in ways that white people living in the 1950s were not. As a child growing up in the South before the civil rights era, O'Connor had partially internalized the racial attitudes and the language passed down to her by her parents and held by the larger culture she was a part of. When Flannery went off to Iowa, she carried the prejudices of her region with her. On one occasion, when visiting writer and fellow southerner John Crowe Ransom came to visit the Workshop, he chose one of O'Connor's stories to read to the class; however, when he came across the word "nigger," he refused to read it aloud and substituted, instead, the more benign term, "Negro." O'Connor was troubled and mystified: "It did spoil the story," she complained to one of her Iowa instructors. "The people I was writing about would never use any other word" (Gooch 124–25). Young Flannery's misunderstanding here is instructive: Ransom had seen more of the world and understood how fraught that term was, even if it was being used for the purposes of accurately capturing the dialogue of poor southern whites. The word, with its power to wound and violate, did not translate outside of the context of the South, and so he chose to omit it.

Interestingly, O'Connor would enter into this same discussion with Ransom years later, in 1955, with regard to the publication of "The Artificial Nigger" in *The Kenyon Review*. As editor of the journal, he suggested altering the title, so as to acknowledge the sensibilities of black readers, but O'Connor held out for her original title. In that particular instance, O'Connor, it seems, made a conscious choice based on a clear understanding of the valence of the word. She was willing to risk offense in order to convey the bold, bald racism inherent in the statue that the title names, the same racism that drives her characters and that they need to own. Most critics and readers concur that O'Connor was well aware of how to wield words in her stories and understood the impact of this particular one, especially in the title position. Critical whiteness theory, however, offers another possible angle from which to see O'Connor's decision. As a beneficiary of white privilege, O'Connor could afford to use language that might be offensive to blacks. According to Julie Armstrong, "Her white privilege did allow her to ignore race in ways that African Americans could not. She could defend her story's title to John Crowe Ransom because 'black folks' sensibilities' mattered less to her than authorial preference. O'Connor did not have to confront on a daily basis affronts to *her* racial sensibilities" (82; emphasis Armstrong's). Thus blinded to its effects on others, O'Connor takes advantage of her whiteness and, consciously or unconsciously, upholds the corrupt racist system that gives white people power to use language that demeans blacks.

Though she would remain, at least to some extent, unaware of this subtle racial dynamic, it does seem that after her first run-in with Ransom, O'Connor gained a fuller understanding of the impact and nuances of the word as she traveled north. Living in New York and then in Connecticut, she would observe the ways in which the customs of that country differed from those of her own. It would further sensitize her to the use of the word in her stories. In the interest of verisimilitude, she could not strike it from the vocabulary of her fiction, but it is used almost exclusively by her characters, either in dialogue with others or in interior monologues, and only by the narrator when he/she is channeling the thoughts of the protagonist. The term reflects *their* racism—and all of the suggestions of provincialism, narrow-mindedness, and sin that go with it—not hers. One might cite many examples of this pattern of usage in O'Connor's stories, but one such instance of it occurs in "Revelation," wherein the racist protagonist, Ruby Turpin, uses the term "nigger" freely to describe black people in general and, more particularly, the field hands that work on her farm. The narrator, in marked contrast to Ruby, refers to blacks and to the farm workers consistently as "Negroes." In an especially telling passage, Ruby imagines herself being interrogated by Jesus before her birth, asking her to choose who she might want to become: "There's only two places available to you. You can either be a nigger or white-trash" (*CS* 491). Mrs. Turpin, in her imagination, imputes to Jesus the language that she herself uses to describe blacks and poor whites, demonstrating her ignorance and insensitivity to the fact that these are demeaning terms that Christ, who had such affinity for the poor and dispossessed, would never use. After much begging and pleading to be released from this dreadful choice, Mrs. Turpin concedes, "All right make me a nigger then—but that don't mean a trashy one" (*CS* 491). At this point the narrator concludes the imagined scenario: "And he [Jesus] would have made her a neat clean respectable Negro woman, herself but black" (CS 491). There is considerable nuance here in O'Connor's use of the term "Negro." While it is clear that this is the voice of the narrator, who consistently employs this term, the narrator also seems to be channeling Mrs. Turpin's thoughts. Whereas Ruby almost unfailingly uses the word "nigger" to describe actual black people (except for the occasional use of the term "colored"), here she uses the term "Negro" to refer to her imagined black self. This subtle slippage foreshadows the distance Ruby Turpin will travel in the course of the story from an unconscious but blatant racist who believes in the principles of white supremacy and her own superiority to blacks, to a wounded but wiser woman who perceives God's unequivocal love for all his creatures, black and white alike.

O'Connor's fiction clearly demonstrates attentiveness to the nuances of racially charged language. The letters, however, tell another story. Finding herself living in the South again, O'Connor seemed to adapt, once more, not only to the customs of her native region, but to the language that went with it. What the linguistic customs of that world were are sometimes hard to pin down, and surely they varied to some degree from place to place, but is worth noting that the word was considered impolite by many people in O'Connor's milieu. Middle-class whites with aspirations to gentility did not typically use it, or, at least, used it rarely and only in very particular circumstances. In contrast to O'Connor's frequent use of the word in her correspondence, Eudora Welty seems to have used it in only four instances in the course of more than 2,600 letters, and these particular four letters were all written to the same person, further suggesting the limiting conditions under which she judged it fit to use (Pollack 4).

According to southern writer William Styron, another contemporary of O'Connor, who grew up in tidewater Virginia, "My mother . . . certainly would have thrashed me had she ever heard me use the word 'nigger'" ("This Quiet Dust" 330). This, of course, did not prevent him from using it among his friends (as O'Connor does), and it most likely didn't prevent the adults from using it, either, among themselves. O'Connor scholar Ralph Wood makes a similar observation about his own upbringing in the South: "I never heard my parents . . . use the word; in fact, they explicitly forbade me to use it in the presence of blacks, knowing that it would deeply wound them" (*Christ-Haunted South* 99). Wood's admission adds another layer to the complexity of its usage, implying it to be a word used by white people only in the company of other white people, a term to be used among intimates and familiars, thus marking it as a term white people used as a means of controlling the narrative of who and what black people are. This proves true in O'Connor's case. We know that she and her mother used the term among themselves. In a letter to Elizabeth Hester, Flannery recounts a brief episode in the sometimes adversarial relationship she and Regina shared and concludes by quoting her mother, "You talk just like a nigger and someday you are going to be away from home and do it and people are going to wonder WHERE YOU CAME FROM" (*CW* 989; emphasis O'Connor's). O'Connor doesn't have to explain what her mother means by "talking like a nigger" to her fellow white Georgian: the word is part of the code of speech white people share, as is the understanding of its denotation of an ignorant, unlettered, crude person, marked off as belonging to the most debased and despised of society. The fact that it was regarded as a forbidden word, in some contexts, comparable to a piece of profanity, marks it as transgressive within the culture. Like the curse words people reserve for private use, one uses it only when others cannot overhear it and primarily when one has something to say one feels strongly about.

O'Connor's frequent reference to "niggers" in her letters is an obstacle for the twenty-first-century reader, not because of some sort of liberal piety but because of the vantage point offered by history. Having the benefit of living outside the culture O'Connor writes from, contemporary readers have seen the ways in which the word has been used (and still is used) to victimize black people—to keep African Americans in bondage, first, and then in submission for a century and more after they were officially freed. It is a word that has been struck from polite public speech. It has been interrogated by linguists and artists, comedians and musicians, theologians and philosophers, sociologists and anthropologists, lawyers and judges, scholars of every stamp, and by ordinary people, all in attempt to understand its history, to map its changing denotations and connotations, and to rob it of its power to denigrate and destroy.

One such writer who has famously scrutinized the word is O'Connor's seeming nemesis James Baldwin. In a television interview Baldwin gave in 1963, "The Negro and the American Promise," he sums up what he sees to be the source of the problem in black-white relations in America:

> What white people have to do is try to find out in their own hearts why it was necessary to have a "nigger" in the first place, because I am not a nigger, I'm a man. But if you think I'm a nigger, it means you need him. The question that you've got to ask yourself, the white population of this country has got to ask itself . . . if I'm not the nigger here and you invented him . . . then you've got to find out why. (qtd. in Baldwin, *I Am Not Your Negro* 108–9)

Baldwin's critique speaks not only to the word, but also to the concept behind the word. As is evident in contemporary scholarship about race, colonial Europeans invented the idea of whiteness, established "'white' identity as a mark of social status," and created the category of the nonwhite Other who was deprived of the entitlements and privileges claimed by whites in order to make it more palatable to enslave and otherwise violate the property and personhood of indigenous peoples and Africans (Allen 248–51; Omi and Winant 58). Baldwin's refusal to be consigned to this category and defined by this white man's word is a metaphor for the whole civil rights movement, the insistence on being counted as a human being, on receiving all of the attendant rights accorded a human being under the Constitution, and on the refusal to be ruled by language and practice deliberately designed to diminish and demean African American people. Baldwin lays the problem of race at the doorstep of those who invented it, white people, all of which can be summed up in a single, ugly word. In Shakespeare's *Romeo and Juliet*, Juliet famously poses the question, "What's in a name?" (2.2.43). "Everything," Baldwin would reply.

In his study *Nigger: The Strange Career of a Troublesome Word*, Randall Kennedy provides a condensed history of "the protean n-word," tracing it from its first recorded usage in America in 1619, through its adoption as a term of insult and contempt in the early nineteenth century, through its use in popular culture of the nineteenth and twentieth centuries to ridicule and demean, through its adoption by African Americans who had internalized the racism it conveys, through to its repurposing by contemporary black comedians and hip-hop artists as a means of dismantling its power as a racial epithet (3–44). Kennedy's argument is thorough and nuanced. Rather than calling for a moratorium on the use of the word, as some social critics have, he instead urges care, consideration, and attention to context in its use. Knowledge of its history will help both white people and black to use what has typically been an emotion-charged word thoughtfully, warily, and sparingly.

In their various ways, as outspoken artist and dedicated scholar, both Baldwin and Kennedy urge white Americans to be mindful of and careful with the word O'Connor uses so cavalierly in her letters and, yet, so judiciously in her stories. O'Connor was almost certainly aware of some of this history and of contemporary ideas about race. Multiple sources would have been at her disposal, including the classic study written by her friend and correspondent Thomas Gossett, *Race: The History of an Idea in America* (1963), a groundbreaking work of scholarship that traces the development and discrediting of biological ideas about race, reveals the shoddy basis for theories about the inequality of blacks and whites, and demonstrates race to be a social construct rather than a physical reality. Gossett's opposition to segregation nearly cost him his academic career: his public support of integration in 1958 lead to his suspension from the faculty at Wesleyan College in Macon, Georgia, and earned O'Connor's admiration and respect (Alexander 57). Gossett provides a compelling narrative of the treatment of African Americans throughout our history, from the first arrival of Africans in the colonial era, through the Civil War and world wars, through the era of immigration and anti-immigrant agitation, and through the early years of the civil rights movement, finally bringing the reader to the present moment wherein he was writing, 1963—that pivotal year—which is simultaneously disastrous (the Birmingham boycott, Medgar Evers's murder, John F. Kennedy's assassination) yet also seems poised on the brink of promise (the rise of Martin Luther King Jr. and the March on Washington). Gossett opens his preface stating, "This book is, then, both a history of race theory and a history of bigotry" and concludes with his hope "that this book may help readers understand the cruelty and absurdity of racism" (xxi–xxii). On April 8, 1964, four months before her death, O'Connor writes to Gossett to let him know "I am really enjoying reading your book. Fr. McCown breezed in here yesterday and appropriated the cover. I wouldn't let him have the book lest I never see it again" (*HB* 573).

In fact, it is Fr. James McCown, O'Connor's Jesuit friend and spiritual counselor, whom she mentions in the letter, who introduced Thomas Gossett and his wife, Louise, to O'Connor, inaugurating what would become a warm friendship. McCown was another source of alternative thinking about race and politics who figured in O'Connor's life. In his essay devoted to the unpublished correspondence between O'Connor and McCown, Benjamin Alexander explores the extraordinary relationship between the conservative fiction writer and the liberal priest and describes O'Connor's predicament: "Torn between the social conservatism of her mother and the profound changes introduced by the civil rights movement... she admired individuals on different sides of the racial divide: her mother and other friends were unwilling to challenge segregation, whereas Father McCown, Tom Gossett, Walker Percy, and others were dedicated to ending it" (55). An Alabama native, Fr. McCown was also raised in a culture of racism and paternalism, spoke out against it plainly and regularly, and would eventually excoriate his region for its long practice of racial injustice in his memoir, *God Writes with Crooked Lines*:

> We southerners showered our black domestics with shallow affection then exploited them shamelessly. We claimed really to know blacks, but lived with our own self-serving image of them. We paid them starvation wages, then feigned disappointment when they turned out to be ungrateful or shiftless or thieving.... We kept them from getting a good education, then complained of their ignorance. We forced them to live in slums, and then condemned them for their violence. We read happiness and contentment in their comedy and obsequiousness and then were outraged if they expressed their human dignity. For our own use we stereotyped them and their language and habits. (16)

McCown's account of the collective sins of the South against African Americans is painfully accurate and attests to his heightened sensitivity to the injustices black people endured. It also captures the dysfunctional relationship between blacks and whites, particularly the ways in which the strictures whites historically imposed on African Americans have caused the social ills that blacks are, in turn, blamed for. Though McCown's memoir would not be published until 1990, decades after O'Connor's death, the two friends spoke of the dynamics McCown describes and of the differences between their viewpoints. His words convey his long-held narrative of race relations in the South—words that, coming from a priest and a fellow southerner, carried a special authority and authenticity for O'Connor.

O'Connor's friendship with both Fr. McCown and Thomas Gossett and her admiration for Gossett's work, read as she was dying of lupus, bespeaks her openness to entertaining ideas about race that conflicted with her own to the end of her life. Even as she is undergoing a personal trial by fire in the form of her worsening health and impending mortality, she demonstrates a curiosity in the face of the seemingly intractable difficulties the subject poses and a sympathy with his treatment of African Americans that is not evident in her letters. Again, as with the divide we see in her use of the word "nigger" in her correspondence and in her fiction, we are faced with O'Connor's double-mindedness when it came to the subject of race.

## Jack, Louise, Shot, and the "Locution of the South"

In preparing her edition of the letters, Sally Fitzgerald sees this divide and attempts to prepare the reader for it in her preface and to fend off any suspicions of racism on O'Connor's part:

> In her letters, she uses the prevailing locution of the South as easily, and as unmaliciously, as it often occurs there, among blacks and whites alike. It was simply natural to her in her time and place. And if she did not live to envision and fully dramatize their role in the divine comedy, it was perhaps because it was her well-met responsibility to her gift to give dignity and meaning to the lives of individuals who have far fewer champions, and enjoy considerably less sympathy, and are far lonelier than they. (*HB* xiv)

Though Fitzgerald's attempt to shield her friend from charges of racism is understandable and laudable, her reasoning here is problematic. First, the use of the word as "simply natural to her in her time and place" is an oversimplification, as previous discussion of the term would suggest. In addition, the idea that the "individuals" O'Connor writes about in her fiction, mostly poor southern whites, "have far fewer champions" and "enjoy considerably less sympathy" than African Americans seems a strange assertion. The history of race relations in America, and particularly in the South, would suggest otherwise. In fact, while it's true that poor whites may be reviled as "white trash" by some segments of southern society, black people living in a culture policed by the KKK and lynch law are considerably more lacking in champions and sympathy. There is no one "lonelier" than a black man facing a lynch mob. In addition, some of the most virulent racism and violent behavior toward blacks have traditionally come from that class. O'Connor herself is well aware of this dynamic, wherein the poor need someone worse off than themselves to despise. The so-called "white trash" woman in the waiting room of O'Connor's story "Revelation" clearly reveals her racial pride and her deep-seated contempt for blacks, stating "Two thangs I ain't going to do: love no niggers or scoot down no hog with no hose" (*CS* 494). Her mention of these two despised creatures together in the same breath further suggests equivalence between them, effectively dehumanizing blacks and thereby placing herself higher in her warped version of the great chain of being, a problematic concept O'Connor critiques throughout the story.

In addition to this defense, Fitzgerald tries to account for some of O'Connor's less than sympathetic attitudes toward African Americans expressed in the letters by noting the limited social world Flannery inhabited. The fact is, she knew very few black people, and among the ones she knew best were the uneducated country people who worked for her mother: "Sentimental about no one else, she was equally unsentimental about blacks as individuals. Frequently she was impatient with them, and said so. . . . The blacks on the O'Connor farm were as primitive as some of the whites she wrote about, and they perhaps serve as trees obscuring her view of the social forest" (*HB* xiv). O'Connor's letters are, in fact, full of stories about Jack and Louise Hill and their boarder, Willie "Shot" Manson, who lived in the cabin located near the main house at Andalusia. Maryat Lee and Elizabeth Hester are most frequently the recipients of Flannery's semihumorous stories narrating the adventures of this dysfunctional family. All three of them seemed to have had alcohol problems, overindulged in local moonshine with some frequency, regularly fought among themselves, and were often incapable of doing their work. The connection between their drinking and the constant threat of domestic violence was a real cause for concern. In one such instance, as described by O'Connor and recounted in Fr. McCown's memoir, a quarrel occasioned the brandishing of a shotgun. O'Connor admires her mother's cool head in a situation that she claims would have reduced her to "idiocy": "Now lets [*sic*] not have any more of this unpleasantness. Bring that shotgun over here and leave it" (McCown iii; qtd. in Alexander 55). Indeed, Regina's attitude toward her help is one of patience and noblesse oblige (as was typical of white women of her class). She treats them like children, intervening in their drunken arguments and taking them to the doctor when they are taken ill or injured on the farm (*HB* 442). She goes so far as to initiate driving lessons for Shot and assists him in the process of getting his license. Unfortunately, he returns the favor by being arrested for drunk driving and has to be bailed out of jail, yet Regina responds graciously and does what duty requires her to do (*HB* 222, 224, 592). This paternalism on the part of both Flannery and her mother is yet another enaction of the southern code. It clearly does not denote a relationship of equals. Regina's workers would have regarded the two white women not only as their employers and social superiors, but as their racial superiors as well, treating them with deference. In his biography of O'Connor, Brad Gooch quotes one of Flannery's friends, Leonard Mayhew, a priest from Atlanta who used to visit Andalusia, recounting the interaction among the O'Connor women and their help: "She [Flannery] never said anything racist, but she was patronizing about blacks. Treated them as children. When I was introduced to black workers on the farm, they would take off their hats. I was both a white man and a priest. So they were doing double duty" (334).

Their deference, however, did not keep the farm workers from acting out when they were not under the watchful eye of their employers. In one of the last letters O'Connor wrote to Elizabeth Hester during her final illness on June 27, 1964, Flannery bemoans the incompetence of the staff, and Louise, in particular, after she and her mother return to Andalusia after spending a month in Piedmont Hospital:

> You asked what was done when we came back. Nothing. We left in a hurry without washing the tops of the breakfast pans or the coffeepot and everything was exactly like we left it. Rip Van Winkle didn't have it any different. Not even a glass of ice water to hand. Dust everywhere. The refrigerator full of rotten food. And Louise bowing & scraping and carrying on about how much she had missed us. Regina had told her hurriedly to take care of everything but nothing specific. Anyway even if she had it wouldn't have done any good. They had a month's vacation with pay . . . (*HB* 587)

As the ellipses at the end of the paragraph indicate, there was more to what Flannery had to say. In the sentence that has been omitted from the published letter, O'Connor states "I sho am sick of niggers" (Emory).

Ill and exhausted as she was, the obvious impatience and frustration O'Connor displays in her description of the house is understandable. O'Connor and her mother have arrived home from their month-long ordeal only to find their home in a state of chaos. However, O'Connor's final statement is one that garners no sympathy—a fact Sally Fitzgerald and/or Regina O'Connor clearly knew, otherwise it would not have been omitted from *The Habit of Being*. Flannery's use of the word "niggers" to describe the people who work for her family is surprising and deeply troubling. O'Connor uses the word frequently and facetiously in her correspondence with Maryat Lee (though, as has been noted, even that usage is complex and problematic), but this is the first instance in the letters where she uses it as a form of castigation and in a context wherein she intentionally demeans particular African Americans by invoking the term. Though the use of the word "sho" suggests some effort at wry humor, adopting the idiom of black people in order to make fun of them—or, perhaps, more troublingly, the idiom of white racists—there is no evidence to suggest O'Connor doesn't mean what she says. Had O'Connor stated that she is sick of Louise, Jack, and Shot and their irresponsible behavior, she would likely elicit a sympathetic response, but seeing her reduce people she lives so closely with to a racial epithet is profoundly disappointing.

In her study of "whiteness and the literary imagination," the subtitle of her book *Playing in the Dark*, Toni Morrison notes that the term "nigger" "occupies a territory between man and animal and thus withholds specificity even while marking it" (71). To call a person a "nigger" is to rob him or her of a name, of an identity, and of a sense of belonging to the human family. The term functions as a means of de-humanizing African Americans and denying their dignity. But the use of the term almost always backfires, as it does here, calling the dignity of the speaker into question. In her implication that all blacks are lazy and irresponsible, as "her" farm workers are, and the twin notion that they are the way they are on account of the fact that they are black, we recognize a way of thinking and speaking that is typically racist. O'Connor denies the worth and integrity not only of her employees but also of an entire people, based on stereotypes about their race. One of O'Connor's friends, a monk at the Trappist Monastery of the Holy Spirit in nearby Conyers, confirms O'Connor's use of this language in speech, as well as in her correspondence, and states plainly, "I would call Flannery a cultural racist.... It wasn't that she didn't know they [African Americans] were children of God redeemed by the blood of Christ. Of course she knew that. But the vocabulary she used was typical Southern white" (Gooch 334).

Fitzgerald's defense of O'Connor, then, as the prisoner of her culture's narrowness, serves to shed some light on her thinking about African Americans, but it does not exonerate her. It is likely that contemporary readers and admirers of O'Connor's work, who are citizens living in the post–civil rights era, wish that she might have struggled harder against the prevailing prejudices of her culture, been more judicious with regard to her use of the troubled and troubling "locution of the South" in her speech and letters, and resisted the temptation to use African Americans, already a victimized people, as the butt of jokes in order to tease Maryat Lee. While it is true that such lapses attest to the common condition of finitude all human beings share, these are lapses most readers prefer not to see in the writers to whom they look for wisdom and truth.

## "Natural" versus "Fictive" Discourse: "There Is a Crack in Everything"

It is worth reminding ourselves of the anomaly that as O'Connor is writing these letters in the late 1950s and early 1960s, she is writing the best stories of her life, including those that are most sensitive to the subject of race: "The Displaced Person" (1953), "The Artificial Nigger" (1954), "The Enduring Chill" (1957), "Everything That Rises Must Converge" (1961), "Revelation" (1964), and "Judgement Day" (1964). In his essay "Where Is the Voice Coming From? Flannery O'Connor on Race," Ralph Wood accounts for this bifurcation in her writing by characterizing the ideas about race she expresses in her letters as "opinion" and those in her fiction as expressions of her "convictions." While "opinions are quickly formed and quickly abandoned," "convictions, by contrast, are slowly acquired and firmly maintained," "the public verities upon which we stand, the truths by which we live and die." Given this essential difference, Wood argues, it is necessary "to take Flannery O'Connor's public work much more seriously than her personal letters" as her "thoughtful convictions triumphed over her doubtful opinions" (96–97).

This is a worthwhile distinction, relating to the nature of the content of O'Connor's writing, but it is also worth considering the difference in the means of conveyance of her ideas. When O'Connor is writing a letter she is engaging in a very different genre of communication from when she is crafting a piece of fiction, and the product of each act of writing must be regarded differently as well. In her seminal study of speech-act theory, *On the Margins of Discourse: The Relation of Literature to Language*, Barbara Herrnstein Smith makes the distinction between "natural discourse" and "fictive discourse" (14–40). Natural discourse is defined as "The verbal acts of real persons on particular occasions in response to particular sets of circumstances" (15). Many variables shape natural discourse—physical circumstances, the relationship between the speaker and the listener, the nature of the occasion of communication, and the linguistic community to which speaker and listener belong. Fictive discourse, on the other hand, is not defined as natural utterance, nor as a historically unique verbal act or event, but instead is carefully crafted, represented speech (or writing) governed by conventions very different from those that govern natural discourse (24). In short, natural discourse is the kind of discourse one engages in when one converses with—or writes a letter to—a friend. It is spontaneous, sparked and marked by immediate circumstance, and is therefore tentative and contingent. Fictive discourse, on the other hand, both speaks its meaning and represents it in its very form, a form the creator has labored to create uniquely for the bodying forth of its meaning—the two cannot be separated. It exists apart from circumstance as it actually *creates* the context in which its meanings are located (36). This is the mode O'Connor operates in when she writes fiction. The creative process and the absence of contingency in fictive discourse lend it a power and authority that natural discourse lacks.

This is not to say that the natural discourse O'Connor practices as she engages in her correspondence does not reveal a kind of truth to readers—but that truth is limited, contingent, and difficult for readers to access and determine with any certainty since its context, so essential to its meaning, is not fully available to us. The fictive discourse of O'Connor's stories, on the other hand, is much more accessible as the reader actually participates in the creation of its meaning(s) through the act of interpretation (36). The reader greets and meets O'Connor's art on its own terms. This, perhaps, runs counter to our expectations. We typically assume that private expressions in O'Connor's letters would tell us more about what and how she thinks than the public art of her stories, but given the nature of the two kinds of discourse, fiction seems more reliable than seeming fact. Wood's and Smith's distinctions between the matter and means of O'Connor's expression help the reader to understand some of the forces at work behind the obvious rift between the borderline racist persona evident in some of the letters and the voice of wisdom we often (though don't always) hear behind her fiction. In the end, there is no need to choose one Flannery O'Connor over the other, for the two forms of discourse are expressions of her mind and heart, and in order to fully appreciate her humanity and her art, we need both.

This is not to excuse O'Connor's racial attitudes as expressed in the correspondence or to claim that those attitudes are without consequence. If, by some miraculous suspension of the laws of time and space, we were able to interrogate her on the charge of racism, it is reasonable to believe that she would own up to it, especially with the hindsight of history. O'Connor, in fact, was painfully aware of her limitations and flaws as it was through her knowledge of them that she was able to see the flaws and limitations of her characters. As is typical of the Catholic O'Connor, she couches this confession in theological language:

> I am not a mystic and I do not lead a holy life. Not that I can claim any interesting or pleasurable sins (my sense of the devil is strong) but I know all about the garden variety, pride, gluttony, envy and sloth, and what is more to the point, my virtues are as timid as my

vices. I think sin occasionally brings one closer to God. . . . A working knowledge of the devil can be very well had from resisting him. (*HB* 92)

The stories might be seen as verbal embodiments of those acts of resistance to "the devil" O'Connor engaged in. What the letters tell us is that O'Connor understood evil in the form of racism from the inside, as one who has practiced it, just as surely as she has committed the classic sins she lists. What the stories tell us is that O'Connor struggled to understand racism from a place outside herself, to escape the constraints of natural discourse and to see fictively. To use O'Connor's theological language, writing fiction became a form of penance or atonement, resistance to her own inherent evil tendencies (or sins), and a means of transcending them.

No writer (or human being, for that matter) is a paragon of moral virtue, even those who are most vigilant—and yet, many artists who were, like O'Connor, deeply flawed people have managed to create powerful art that transcends their personal limitations. Given this, perhaps the wisest way to address this contradiction in O'Connor's writing is to let it stand instead of trying to resolve it, and allow each mode of expression (the correspondence and the fiction, the opinion and the conviction, the natural and the fictive) to illuminate the other. Rather than attempting to mend the fissures in the facade, we might probe them, follow them, and find the patterns they make. In the late Canadian poet Leonard Cohen's fictive words, "There is a crack in everything. That's how the light gets in" ("Anthem").

# 3 / Theology, Religion, and Race: Constant Conversion and the Beginning of Vision

Flannery O'Connor's social and political milieu, as characterized in the preceding chapter, certainly helped to shape her views on race, but an equally powerful influence on her understanding of race relations was O'Connor's theological vision. As an observant Catholic, an avid reader of a broad range of theological writers, and a member of an institutional church that was itself embattled and conflicted with regard to the role of African Americans in American society and the life of the church, O'Connor entertained a variety of possible solutions to the problem of race—possibilities she would further explore in her fiction and her correspondence.

In his essay "Where Is the Voice Coming From? Flannery O'Connor on Race," Ralph Wood poses the question implicitly raised in the previous chapter, "What made Flannery O'Connor change her racial views so drastically from the liberal sympathies expressed in her earlier stories to the position of a racial gradualist suggested by her mature work?" He posits an answer:

> I suspect that O'Connor undertook an about-face on the race question for theological rather than sociological reasons. . . . O'Connor changed her mind because she recovered her faith. She discovered that she was a radical and not a nominal Catholic. . . . What this restoration of religious conviction revealed to O'Connor is that the liberal estimate of human nature is mistaken in the most fundamental way. It ignores the enduring reality of Original Sin, especially in its power to infect the racially righteous no less than the racially sinful. (99–100)

Wood's assessment offers a reasonable rationale for the gradual development of O'Connor's thought with regard to race; however, it is incomplete in that it attempts to separate the theological from the sociological, thus creating a bifurcation that is not reflected in O'Connor's thinking or writing, as this chapter will demonstrate. But first it is important to acknowledge that her relationship to her faith certainly underwent changes in the course of her education and experience—significant changes, in fact, that are borne out in her journal and letters and dramatized in some of her stories.

Though always an observant Catholic, O'Connor found her faith sorely tried by the experience of attending school at Iowa. In his introduction to O'Connor's *Prayer Journal*, the diary she kept while a student at the Workshop, William Sessions suggests that O'Connor initiated the journal in response to the "new influences" and "intellectual joys" she was experiencing, but also in response to the deep questions and skepticism they engendered in her. Granted, during her time at Iowa, O'Connor attended Mass almost daily at St. Mary's Church and later would attest that it helped assuage her sense of alienation: "As soon as I went in the door I was home" (*HB* 422). She also wrote to her mother every day, as she would continue to do during the next few years when she was living away from her, as another means of maintaining a connection with her regional and religious identity, as well as her family. But the two lives she was leading—that of a faithful Catholic and that of a student in a secular university characterized largely by a culture of unbelief—were brought into conflict with one another on a daily basis. The journal allowed Flannery space within which to create a "rare colloquy" between the two worlds and two decidedly different frames of mind (Sessions, Introduction vii).

O'Connor's fear of losing her faith was well grounded, based in her own precocious self-knowledge: "I dread, Oh Lord, losing my faith. My mind is not strong. It is prey to all sorts of intellectual quackery. I do not want it to be fear which keeps me in the church . . . I want to love to be in [it]" (*Prayer Journal* 5). Brilliant as she was, O'Connor understood the temptations of the intellect. Added to this temptation was her ambition to be a writer. We see her wrestling with her pride throughout the journal in passages such as this one:

> Dear God, tonight it is not disappointing because you have given me a story. Don't let me ever think, dear God that I was anything but the instrument for your story—just like the typewriter was mine. . . .
> When I think of all I have to be thankful for I wonder that you don't

just kill me now because you've done so much for me already and I haven't been particularly grateful. (10–11)

O'Connor's confession of her ingratitude (a foreshadowing of the confession of the bright but spiritually wayward young protagonist in "A Temple of the Holy Ghost," a story she would write years later), attests to her developing sense of her considerable capacities as a writer and the power exerted on others by her work. With this discovery comes exhilaration, certainly, and joy—but it is also frightening, since she is uncertain of the source of this power. In this particular entry, she seems certain that God or the Holy Spirit is responsible for her work, and that she is God's instrument. Though this may seem a bit grandiose, coming from an apprentice writer who has penned a couple of stories, it demonstrates the young O'Connor's sense that her work plays an important role in the drama of her salvation. Much as she is given to joking, O'Connor is dead earnest when it comes to her writing. This is consonant with other entries wherein she pleads with God to make her a good writer, to send her a story, to enable her to get her work published, and to enable "Christian principles" to permeate her work—but very often these entries betray a young woman in a state of desolation, aware of her weakness, ingratitude, and sinfulness. The latter sentiment reaches a climax in the penultimate entry of the journal, dated September 25, 1945: "What I am asking for is really very ridiculous. Oh Lord, I am saying, at present I am a cheese, make me a mystic, immediately" (38).

This plea for a holiness she feels she lacks, written by a twenty-two-year-old in the throes of a crisis of faith, is both humorous and poignant. As in her letters, essays, and stories, O'Connor blends the tragic and the comic as it is essential to her vision. Her sense of abandonment is redeemed by her ever-present sense of her own absurdity and, yet, her hope that God can and will empower her to be the faithful servant she cannot be on her own attests to her faith. The poignancy of her plea is underscored by the final journal entry, made the following day, in which she concedes defeat in the spiritual battle she has been waging within and against herself: "My thoughts are so far away from God. He may as well not have made me.... Today I have proved myself a glutton—for Scotch oatmeal cookies and erotic thought. There is nothing left to say of me" (39). Fortunately, O'Connor's prediction of her spiritual demise did not prove true. Her faith would survive the assaults made by her education at Iowa (1945–48), by her sojourn among (mostly) unbelieving writers at Yaddo (1948–49), and her dispiriting six-month stay in New York City (March–August 1949). O'Connor's fortuitous friendship with Catholic convert Robert Lowell, forged at Yaddo, with devout Catholics Sally and Robert Fitzgerald, and her relocation to their rural retreat in Ridgefield, Connecticut, on September 1, 1949, came at a key moment in her life, as she was trying to finish her first novel and (still) struggling to reconcile her spiritual life with her creative one.

Writing to her Iowa friend Robie Macauley, O'Connor was exultant in her new setting, announcing, "Me and Enoch are living in the woods in Connecticut with the Robert Fitzgerald's," and betraying the degree to which her fictional characters had taken on a life of their own, making them as vivid and present to her as her flesh-and-blood friends (*CW* 886). In the course of her sixteen months in the woods, O'Connor would bring *Wise Blood* to near completion, sign a contract with her new publisher (and fellow Catholic) Robert Giroux, and develop the deep and abiding friendship with the Fitzgerald family that would last until her death. They were in many ways the happiest months of her life. O'Connor's new routine was as regular as it is enviable as a model for a writer's—and, particularly, a Catholic writer's—life. She rose early to attend Mass at Sacred Heart Church in Georgetown, four miles away, with one of the Fitzgeralds, ate breakfast with the family, and then retired to the quiet of her apartment over their garage to work for four hours on her novel. At noon, she would eat lunch and walk the half-mile to the mailbox to post her daily letter to her mother. In the afternoon, she would help oversee the Fitzgerald children, and at the end of the day, once the children were in bed and Robert returned from his day of teaching at Sarah Lawrence in Westchester County, New York, the adults would mix a pitcher of martinis, share an evening meal, and talk late into the night about their common passions—literature and religion.

O'Connor treasured these conversations. They were as literary as any she had experienced at Yaddo, but the added dimension of bringing Catholic writers into the conversation grounded their love of books and their practice as writers in their faith. They circulated books by Lord Acton, the Catholic historian; John Henry Newman; and Fr. Philip Hughes, whose history of the Reformation in England O'Connor much admired. In addition, Robert Fitzgerald shared O'Connor's conviction that good literature fed the soul as surely as it fed the heart and the mind. They shared their favorite books and authors—Flannery suggested that they read books by southern writers such as William Faulkner's *As I Lay Dying*, and Robert gave Flannery drafts of his working translation of *Oedipus Rex*, a play she had not yet read and whose terrifying conclusion would inspire her to reshape the events of *Wise Blood*—namely, Hazel Motes's blinding of himself with quicklime, one of several penitential acts he performs in atonement for the murder he has committed. The action is an echo of the failed attempt at self-blinding on the part of the false prophet (and Motes's nemesis) Asa Hawks, only Motes succeeds, effectively discrediting his rival; but it is also a corollary to Oedipus's blinding of himself. Making the connection between O'Connor's gestating novel and Fitzgerald's translation of the play, the reader comes to recognize it for the brilliant trope that it is—Motes enacting both Oedipus's and his own recognition of his primal sin, its irrevocable nature, and his near despair.

Clearly, all of this conversation, in addition to her reading, fueled O'Connor's writing and fired her imagination, deepening her vision as well as her faith and enabling her to work at an unaccustomed pace: "The novel is going well, almost fast," she—a typically slow and deliberate writer—wrote to a friend on October 31, 1949 (*HB* 17). For a brief time, O'Connor seemed to have found the ideal life among friends and fellow Catholics, all members of the community of believers often referred to, in the parlance of the era, as The Mystical Body of Christ. As time passed, their relationship would continue to deepen. In May of the following year, O'Connor stood as godmother to the Fitzgeralds' third child, Maria Juliana, along with the infant's godfather and her publisher, Robert Giroux. "She was now one of the family," Robert Fitzgerald observed in his introduction to the posthumous publication of *Everything That Rises Must Converge*, "and no doubt the coolest and funniest one" (xvi). They had become family in a religious sense as well as a personal one. The young woman who had wrestled with her doubts in Iowa five years earlier recovered her faith and her faith community in the Fitzgeralds.

O'Connor did not experience reconversion to Catholicism, however, solely as a joy. When the sudden onset of lupus sent her back to Georgia in December 1950, she embarked on a journey that would take the form of a *via crucis*, an agonizing experience that would both challenge and confirm her faith. As a result of the fierce attack of the disease she suffered on the train ride back to Georgia from Connecticut, O'Connor spent eight months in Emory University Hospital in Atlanta, suffering from raging fevers, inflamed joints, rashes, and severe sweats, typical manifestations of lupus that would eventually be abated only by means of high doses of steroids. When the original diagnosis of rheumatoid arthritis was found to be mistaken and the diagnosis of lupus was confirmed, Regina chose to withhold the dreadful news, fearing it would be devastating for Flannery to learn she had the same disease that killed her father when she was only fifteen. Regina did inform Sally Fitzgerald of Flannery's true condition, while she chose to let her daughter live with the fiction that she had arthritis. Seventeen months later, on a summer visit with the Fitzgeralds,

O'Connor would finally learn the truth from Sally. Brad Gooch relates Sally's recollection of the fateful moment:

> Reacting to this sudden revelation, Flannery slowly moved her arm from the car door down into her lap, her hand visibly trembling.... "Well, that's not good news," Flannery said, after a few silent, charged moments. "But I can't thank you enough for telling me.... I thought I had lupus, and I thought I was going crazy. I'd a lot rather be sick than crazy." (215)

Though Regina might have spared O'Connor the sensation of "going crazy," she did give her daughter the gift of time—time to gradually adjust to the new geographical, physical, psychic, and spiritual space she had arrived at. As O'Connor was enduring her first bout with what she thought was arthritis, she was hopeful of her eventual recovery. Believing she would be returning to her literary life in New York and Connecticut undoubtedly gave her the strength and drive to get well. It also enabled her to stay focused on her work. Gravely ill, O'Connor essentially finished her novel as she lay on what might well have proven her deathbed—a circumstance that foreshadowed events that would unfold fourteen years later, as the last weeks before her death she would labor intensely to complete three of her finest stories, "Revelation," "Parker's Back," and "Judgement Day."

Throughout the years of her illness, O'Connor's fiction would serve as a proving ground for the reality that she herself struggled with, both early and late. In a letter to Elizabeth Hester, O'Connor describes the almost manic state she was in as she revised the final chapters of *Wise Blood*:

> I was five years writing that book, and up to the last I was sure it was a failure and didn't work. When it was finished I came down with my energy-depriving ailment and began to take cortisone in large doses and cortisone makes you think night and day until I suppose the mind dies of exhaustion if you are not rescued. I was, but during this time I was more or less living my life and H. Mote's too and as my disease affected the joints, I conceived the notion that I would eventually become paralyzed and was going blind and that in the book I had spelled out my own course, or that in the illness I had spelled out the book. (*HB* 117–18)

Fueled by steroids, O'Connor experienced the ferocious energy necessary for her to rewrite the story (in longhand, no less) she had labored at so long, but she also experienced the terrifying sensation of identifying with her obsessed, Christ-haunted, and pathological protagonist, Hazel Motes.

Both the creator and her creature were undergoing a baptism-by-fire, both in physical and spiritual terms, suffering the privations and desolations that, paradoxically, bring one to faith. O'Connor poured into her novel all of her own agonies—not only her disease, but also her displacement. As Paul Elie observes, "Coming home for O'Connor was a crucifixion, with all the term implies. In her illness, and the loneliness it brought, she saw the suffering of Christ, whose suffering was the model for the suffering of Hazel Motes" (193). Eventually, Hazel would emerge not only saved, but a saint. O'Connor would emerge chastened, reconverted to her own faith, shadowed by death but grateful to be alive.

Two years before the onset of her disease, on August 17, 1948, O'Connor had written to Elizabeth Ames, the director of Yaddo, "Were it not for my mother, I could easily resolve not to see Georgia again" (qtd. in Gooch 156). Nine years later, O'Connor would acknowledge in a letter to her friend and fellow writer Cecil Dawkins the grace of both her return to the South and even the horrific illness that occasioned it: "I stayed away from the time I was 20 until I was 25 with the notion that the life of my writing depended on my staying away. I would certainly have persisted in that delusion had I not got very ill and had to come home. The best of my writing has been done here" (*CW* 1037). Though she may have been dragged back to Georgia against her will, O'Connor found there what she had been searching for: the material for her fiction. She became an avid observer of her circumscribed world. With her eye for detail and with her fine ear for idiom, she watched and listened to the people of Milledgeville, to her mother and the members of her large Catholic family, and to her neighbors, including the Stevens family, her mother's dairyman, his wife, and their two daughters, who would provide models for her of the white farmworkers featured in her stories. She would capture images, expressions, and snippets of speech that would later find their way into her narrative and dialogue. She would also study the newspapers for interesting local stories, scenarios, and names of characters (Gooch 201). O'Connor discovered in the Georgia countryside a world full of folks who would populate the world of her fiction. This included the African American people she interacted with—including Jack and Louise Hill and Shot Manson—and the characters they would become. The southern code of manners and the relationship between blacks and whites peculiar to the South were reintroduced into her life, no longer as conditions to be taken for granted, as they surely had been when she was a child and a teenager, but as circumstances she was seeing anew from the vantage point of an adult, of a newly recommitted Catholic, and of a writer.

In his assessment of the development of O'Connor's ideas on race quoted at the start of this chapter, Ralph Wood argues that the gradual shift in her thinking is due to "theological rather than sociological reasons" (99). While it is clear that the theological impulse is primary in O'Connor, her theology cannot be separated from her experience of the sociological, a truth made evident in the preceding biographical narrative. Rather than the "either-or" situation Wood posits, any account of O'Connor's influences is best summed up as "both-and." The theological does not exist as pure abstraction but instead works itself out in sociological and historical reality. O'Connor's Catholicism is a lived faith and her theology radically incarnational. This inevitable commingling of the theological, or doctrinal abstraction, with the sociological, or concrete experience, will be made more explicit in a brief overview of her theological vision and, again, later in the chapter in the discussion of O'Connor's relationship to the Church—a Church that is erected on a theological foundation but manifests itself as a social institution. O'Connor's theology informs her vision of the world but also exists in tension with it, and it is from such tension that her fiction emerges.

## Incarnational, Anagogical, and Analogical: O'Connor's Theological Vision

This account of O'Connor's recovery of her faith gives us a sense of where O'Connor was in her life, in psychic and spiritual terms, when she was writing her stories and how she arrived at that fraught and propitious place. No writer works in a vacuum. Circumstance shapes the products of one's imagination as surely as it shapes one's mind, heart, and way of seeing the world. To understand how O'Connor regards and treats race in her fiction, it is necessary to understand her angle of vision and the lens through which she observes her subject. Her newfound theological vision was hard won, emerging from a crucible of suffering. It was also a vision now founded in the certainty of her own death, arrived at by age twenty-five, a reality many human beings never fully grasp. O'Connor once stated in an interview, "I'm a born Catholic and death has always been brother to my imagination" (Magee 107). While this is true—seeing the tortured corpus hung from the crucifix on the walls of her home and church from infancy, the Catholic child bears witness to death very young—and while it is also true that the death of O'Connor's father ushered in a dreadful renewal of that knowledge of death ten years before she was struck by lupus, grappling with the fact of her own inevitable mortality on a daily basis served to enlarge her vision, insisting that she see events in light of eternity. This includes both the small daily events going on around her, the ones she recorded with such fidelity in her stories, as well as the large historic events taking place on a national and international scale. This simultaneous largeness and smallness, this cosmic breadth and this focused attention to minute particulars, characterizes O'Connor's vision. The theological permeates her perception and informs her moral and aesthetic vision. O'Connor referred to this as "anagogical vision," a term borrowed from medieval scriptural exegesis, which she defines as a "kind of vision that is able to see different levels of reality in one image or one situation," one of those levels of reality being "the Divine life and our participation in it" (*MM* 72). Of the four levels of possible meaning imputed to a text—the literal, the typological, the moral, and the anagogical—the latter concerns itself with last things, namely Death, Judgment, Heaven, and Hell, and, ultimately, the mystical. Thus, when O'Connor creates a scenario—the conflict between black and white people on a city bus or the terror of a white grandfather and his grandson when they get lost in the black neighborhoods of Atlanta—there is much more at stake than contemporary racial politics. While these circumstances serve as the concrete material of her stories, she urges the reader to see beyond them, and beyond race, to the ultimate meanings and mysteries the characters and their actions body forth: "The fiction writer is interested in individuals, not races; he knows that good and evil are not apportioned along racial lines and when he deals with topical matters, if he is any good, he sees the long run through the short run" (Magee 109).

In addition to O'Connor's anagogical vision, a term that is primarily literary in impulse, her vision can also be described as radically incarnational and analogical, theologically oriented terms that convey her belief in divine immanence in the creation and her belief in her role as an artist to make that vision apparent to the reader:

> The novelist is required to create the illusion of a whole world with believable people in it, and the chief difference between the novelist who is an orthodox Christian and the novelist who is merely a naturalist is that the Christian novelist lives in a larger universe. He believes that the natural world contains the supernatural. And this doesn't mean that his obligation to portray the natural is less; it means it is greater. (*MM* 175)

O'Connor's imaginative project was to embody the deep mystery of human experience as it is manifest in the visible world. As a Catholic, she believed in the goodness of creation, as opposed to its corruption (a belief shared by nihilists and some Protestants, especially those most closely allied with the traditional teachings of Luther and Calvin that the world is marred by sin), and she also believed in the abiding presence of evil: "Catholics believe that all creation is good and that evil is the wrong use of good and that without Grace we use it wrong most of the time" (*HB* 144). Both human nature and the world are, in fact, a messy amalgam of the two, or, to use a familiar metaphor, both serve as battlegrounds for the cosmic forces of good and evil that come into violent conflict around and within us. However, artists do not traffic in abstractions. All of this heady theology has to be channeled in the work of a fiction writer into the particular and the real:

> Whatever the novelist sees in the way of truth must first take on the form of his art and must be embodied in the concrete and human ... because every mystery that reaches the human mind, except in the final stages of contemplative prayer, does so by way of the senses. Christ didn't redeem us by a direct intellectual act, but became incarnate in human form, and he speaks to us now through the mediation of a visible Church. All this may seem a long way from the subject of fiction, but it is not, for the main concern of the fiction writer is with mystery as it is incarnated in human life. (*MM* 176)

Mystery is the *summum bonum* O'Connor is always after—not solving it, not explaining it, not apologizing for it, but observing it, bringing it to life in language, and making it accessible to her fellow human beings. She takes her cue for this from the Incarnation, casting God as the ultimate fiction-maker and herself—along with all other good fiction writers, whether they are aware of it or not—as disciple.

O'Connor was deeply read in theology and found the work of particular theologians to be helpful to her in shaping her moral and aesthetic vision. Among the most influential writers she read was philosopher Fr. William Lynch, whose book *Christ and Apollo* championed the model of Christ as artist. Sarah Gordon summarizes aptly the vision O'Connor found so compelling in Lynch: "Just as the descent of Christ into history and time redeems both history and time and provides the analogical model for the artist, the artist must of necessity be immersed in the particulars of place and time in order to ascend to vision" (141–42). That immersion is total, encompassing the ugly and the beautiful, goodness and evil, the tragic and the comic, and it is only through immersion in the most basic blood-and-bones business of being human that one learns anything about humanity. Like Dante, who sends his pilgrim to hell before he can ascend to paradise, Lynch understood that "the way up is the way down" (Lynch 27–28). Clearly, this is a lesson O'Connor learned well, as evident from her fiction, stories in which gruesome, ugly, and violent events are somehow able to lead people to holiness.

Another thinker who exerted a powerful influence on O'Connor's vision was French paleontologist, theologian, and philosopher, Fr. Teilhard de Chardin (who, like Lynch, was a Jesuit). Teilhard was a controversial figure during his own lifetime. Due to some early writings in which he expressed ideas that seemed to run contrary to Church teaching—including an understanding of the natural world that seemed to border on the pantheistic—he was forbidden to publish any of his philosophical works. This, however, did not deter him from writing them nor did it deter his avid followers from distributing them without Vatican approval. Though O'Connor was a faithful Catholic in just about every way, her intellectual curiosity sometimes got the better of her devotion to Church teaching, so she read and reviewed the writings of Teilhard without pangs of conscience. It also helped that she had a Jesuit as a spiritual director. Fr. James McCown frequently gave O'Connor permission when she asked if she could read books that appeared on the *Index Librorum Prohibitorum*. Teilhard's vision is particularly consequential in terms of O'Connor's ideas about race and politics. In his signature work, *The Divine Milieu*, Teilhard describes the process of human and natural evolution as a process of "divinization." Richard Giannone summarizes the ideas in Teilhard's writing that O'Connor absorbed:

> The entire universe is, and always has been, in perpetual evolution toward cosmic convergence into a single whole. The air, the earth, humankind—everything—are headed toward a unitive perfection. That end is union with God through God's Son. The organic surge culminates with Christ manifesting himself in all things. Christ is the Omega for everything. His pervasive presence makes matter divine; this divinization of the physical, the *Parousia*, signals the fulfillment of convergence and the end of time. . . . Teilhard is convinced that humanity, for all the evolved growth it has attained, remains to be completed in physical nature and that suffering, epitomized by the crucifixion, holds the secret of convergence. (157)

This process of divinization is happening without conscious human agency. In fact, most of the consequential events that occur in the world and in the individual life of a human being take place while we are passive. As commentator Fr. Thomas King notes in his introduction to a recent translation of *The Divine Milieu*,

All of us were passive through the long ages in which the human genome was developed, passive as we were formed in the womb, and passive as our body grew—our passivities are immeasurably wider and deeper than our activities. We were passive as the forces of evolution brought us to life and growth, and passive as the same forces draw us to diminishment and death. (xx)

Human activity does not bring about the *Parousia*—only God's work in the world can accomplish this grand end. Given this theological vision, it is easy to see why O'Connor would find the efforts of civil rights activists to be a form of folly, at best, and a collective act of overweening pride, at worst. The puny efforts of human beings cannot bring about the victory of good over evil, and to witness people trying to achieve this constitutes both a sad and comic enterprise. O'Connor's most celebrated story that deals with race—as well as her final collection of stories—takes its title from Teilhard's work, "Everything That Rises Must Converge," and depicts this folly. The main characters in the story—the pseudo-liberal Julian, his racist mother, and the angry black woman—all take warring stances on the race question and are brought into violent collision. Their convergence, however, is a dark and disastrous one, not the beatific one God has in store for humankind.

## A White Church and a Slow Church

This brief overview of O'Connor's theological vision provides, perhaps, some possible answers to the perplexing questions raised in the previous chapter about why O'Connor was not passionately engaged in the civil rights movement. While she knew these events to be important, she saw them in the light of the three Christian truths that governed her radically Christian vision: the Fall, the Redemption, and the Judgment (*MM* 185). With such an understanding of the course of human history and of the inevitable dynamic of every human life, grand and mythic in scale, one fights against the impulse to simplify and sentimentalize. O'Connor refused to demonize one side of a political debate and idealize the other: She saw sin and human error in operation on both sides of the political divide, where they simply took different forms. Granted, most of us would argue that there is far greater sin and human error evident on the side of the implicitly racist resisters to integration than on the side of the angry and self-righteous reformers, but O'Connor would argue they are alike in kind if not in degree, and that both are deserving of censure. This is the kind of vision and discernment that Ralph Wood suggests is at work in O'Connor in his assessment of the development of her racial views. While he is surely wise in identifying her faith as a key factor in her portrayal of racial conflict—as it was a key factor for all of her thinking and writing—it is also necessary to look beyond her theology at the incarnate, sociological reality of the pre–Vatican II Church to which O'Connor found herself pledging fealty.

The Church Flannery O'Connor believed in was not the politically left-leaning, social-justice-hungry American Catholic Church of Thomas Merton, Dorothy Day, and, eventually, the Berrigan brothers. Regarding Day, in particular, O'Connor had little sympathy with "the pacifist-anarchist business" the Catholic Worker professed (*HB* 173). She also objected to Day's meddling in matters that she believed were not hers to meddle in. O'Connor makes fun of Day in one of her letters after a terrifying incident wherein Day and some of her Catholic Workers came south from New York City to Koinonia, the interracial utopian community in Americus, Georgia, in a show of solidarity with their African American and white integrationist members, a visit that erupted in violence on the part of the locals. Upon learning that "D.D. had been to Koinonia and had been shot at," O'Connor confesses,

> All my thoughts on this subject are ugly and uncharitable—such as: that's a mighty long way to come to get shot at, etc. I admire her very much. I still think of the story about the Tennessee hillbilly who picked up his gun and said, "I'm going to Texas to fight fuhmuh rights." I hope that to be of two minds about some things is not to be neutral. (*HB* 218)

O'Connor expresses similar disdain for northern liberal integrationists who come to the South to pontificate about how southerners ought to handle their race problems frequently in her letters, but in this case, because Day is Catholic, her critique is especially sharp as well as telling. Day is motivated by her faith as well as by her political leanings, by the Church's contention that all human beings, black and white, are loved by God and equal in his eyes. Day, unlike O'Connor, is not "of two minds" about the race question or about what actions one ought to take. O'Connor is clearly aware of this difference between herself and her fellow Catholic, begrudgingly admitting to Day's holiness—a holiness that would, eventually, put her on the path toward canonization. She sees her own weakness here, admits to her radical ambivalence, and expresses "hope" that her way of thinking and course of (in)action does not make her morally culpable.

The truth is, though, that O'Connor's position with regard to integration was more in keeping with the actions of the pre–Vatican II Church than Day's. The Catholic Church had long been a segregated institution. The history of relations between white Catholics and black people in America, both North and South, was fraught from the start. During the colonial era, the Church actively participated in the slave trade as a number of priests in religious orders were permitted to own slaves, the most recent incident bespeaking this shameful history that has come to light being that of the Jesuit founders of Georgetown University who sold slaves they owned in order to obtain funds to support the University. Catholics shared the same cultural assumption of black inferiority that other white Americans held. This was evident among educated and noneducated Catholics, and it took an especially virulent and destructive form among immigrant Catholics, especially the Irish who emigrated to the United States in such large numbers in the nineteenth and early twentieth centuries. As historian Cyprian Davis observes, this disdain for and resentment of African Americans emanated from the top of the hierarchy. New York's Archbishop John Hughes (1787–1864) publicly expressed his views on slavery, stating that "the lot of slaves in the South was not half as miserable as that of the exploited Irish workers in the North," and, acceding to the argument made by white Christians for centuries to justify enslaving Africans, that "their condition of being sold as slaves was much better than the alternative," the supposedly savage life they had been rescued from in their native land (Davis 60). The immigrant Irish workers felt this tension between themselves and the free blacks they competed with in the North for jobs given the economic reality that "both the Irish and the free black population in the North were on the bottom rung of the social and the economic ladders" (Davis 58). These conditions led, in part, to the infamous draft riots in New York City in the summer of 1863, a rebellion staged, in part, against enforced military conscription which poor Irish were not able to buy themselves out of. For four days Irish Catholics brutalized the African American population, burning property and carrying out lynchings and the systematic murder of women and children. In a fine piece of irony, it was Archbishop Hughes who was called upon to control the rioters, his public speeches calling for peace proving to be one of his last acts before he died in 1864 (Davis 58).

After the Civil War, the history of black people in the Catholic Church was one of constant struggle and agitation on the part of black Catholics for recognition, equal opportunities for education, participation in the life of the Church, and leadership roles. While there were bishops in various parts of the country during the nineteenth century, particularly Bishop W. H. Gross of Savannah in 1884 and Bishop John Ireland of St. Paul, Minnesota, in 1891, who spoke out against "the color line" that kept up "a wall of separation between whites and blacks" and insisted that "the Negro be our equal in the enjoyment of all political rights of the citizen" (Osborne 25), these voices were few and largely ignored. The Church was ill equipped to handle the race problem, given its deep cultural roots. In fact, as historian William Osborne notes, "the church itself was partly responsible for the problem. It had, for generations, held up eternal salvation as the reward for enduring the misery of slavery. Unwittingly, it put theological props under the evil" (77).

This is the history of the Church O'Connor inherited. Black Catholics in America had always worshipped separately, and the legacy of that segregation was evident in the reality of her religious practice. It is unlikely that O'Connor knew any black Catholics in Milledgeville (she knew very few white ones, for that matter, since Catholics constituted such a small minority of the population), though she may have observed some in the more Catholic city of Savannah when she was growing up. The few black Catholics who may have lived in middle Georgia would not be permitted to attend Mass at Sacred Heart Church with Flannery, Regina, and the Cline family. It is remarkable to think that O'Connor, who believed fervently in the communion of all Catholics by virtue of belonging to the Mystical Body of Christ, would never receive the Eucharist with an African American. The Church she belonged to was, effectively, a white church. She would have encountered no black priests dispensing the sacraments, no black sisters teaching in white schools, and no black parishioners sitting in the pews. This is an absence O'Connor, along with other white Catholics, would have taken for granted, despite the fact that it ran counter to the teaching of the universal Church. They were accustomed to the gap between the beliefs promulgated by the institutional church and the observance of them.

This gap became particularly evident to Catholics during the civil rights movement, posing the opportunity for the Church to extricate itself from the evil of institutional racism once and for all. In 1958, the American bishops issued a formal statement addressing racism as a moral issue and taking an unequivocal stand against it, stating that "discrimination based on the accidental fact of race or color . . . cannot be reconciled with the truth that God has created all men with equal rights and equal dignity" and concluding that "segregation cannot be reconciled with the Christian view of our fellow man" (Davis 255; Osborne 13). Even before this pronouncement, some forward looking bishops in both the North and the South made public statements decrying segregation. As early as 1929, New York's Cardinal Patrick Hayes declared that "every Catholic church is wide open for anyone who wishes to enter for devotional purposes.... [Segregation] does not represent the attitude nor the spirit of the Catholic Church" (Osborne 33). Meanwhile, in the more rigidly segregated South, Archbishop Joseph Rummel of New Orleans from the beginning of his administration of the diocese in 1935 actively worked to dismantle Jim Crow's influence in the Church, directing that signs indicating "For Colored" be removed from the churches, insisting "that Negroes were to have access to any Catholic church in the diocese" and that priests should "avoid anything which would discourage or impede Negro participation in the life of the Church" (Osborne 74).

Despite this strong language from the hierarchy and these symbolic gestures on the part of Churchmen, however, there was little progress toward actual desegregation of Catholic churches and, more particularly, Catholic schools. Even though some individual pastors embraced the American bishops' formal statement and tried to put it into practice, their efforts suffered from the same resistance (albeit not as violent) on the part of white Catholics that efforts to integrate the public schools met. In addition, local law enforcement, especially in the South, could not and would not lend aid to the Church to protect people against any potential violence. Nonetheless, these attempts took place both throughout the South and close to home. In February 1961, Bishop Hyland of Atlanta joined the bishops of Savannah and Charleston in a public announcement that parochial schools would be integrated. Amid the controversy that ensued, white families withdrew their children from the schools at the prospect of black children in the classroom, and the schools were forced to renege on their promise. Ultimately, Catholic schools in the South would not be integrated until after the public schools (Schroeder 68). In general, lay Catholics were slow to respond to the clarion call of the civil rights movement. As Cyprian Davis points out, "By and large, Catholics, either black or white, were not in the forefront of the civil rights movement or among the leadership of the protest organizations. Moreover, the notion that it was unseemly for either clergy or religious to engage in public spectacles like demonstrations was especially strong among Catholics" (265). This would not change until March 1965, seven months after O'Connor's death, when Martin Luther King Jr. called on all of the nation's clergy to participate in the march in Selma, Alabama. "The response of white Catholic priests and sisters was enormous," as the American Catholic conscience was finally awakened by King, though there would still be holdouts, particularly in the South, as evidenced by "the disapproval of the bishop of Mobile-Birmingham" (Davis 256).

Thus, the white Church stayed white in O'Connor's lifetime, but she had inklings that it would not always remain so. In a letter to Maryat Lee written on November 9, 1962, she discusses the changes that are gradually taking place in the South, writing, "My mama . . . [is] accepting all the changes in her stride. The Church makes itself felt along those lines. I take several Catlic [sic] papers which are always yapping about racial justice. Actually *I* am the conservative in this family. Strictly a Kennedy conservative. I like the way that man is running the country" (*HB* 499; emphasis O'Connor's).

As ever, it is wise to consider the context of the letter, given the antagonistic role Flannery liked to play with Maryat in their correspondence, but even so we see on O'Connor's part a resistance to what she perceives as the left-leaning Church's liberalism. It is noteworthy that she casts herself as a devotee of Kennedy, who, as the first Catholic president ever elected, achieved that milestone by assuring nervous anti-Catholic Americans that his primary allegiance would be to his country rather than to his Church. O'Connor presents both herself and Kennedy, who at the time subscribed to a reluctantly gradualist position on integration, in opposition to the church's more progressive stance, choosing to ignore the annoying "yapping" of the Catholic press. It is also well to remember that the Church as a whole was starting to undergo enormous changes at the time O'Connor is writing. The Second Vatican Council (1962–1965) had officially convened a month before and begun the process of reassessing the role of the Church in the modern world. O'Connor would not live to see most of the sweeping changes the Council would institute, but she was witness to the inauguration of a new era of Catholic activism, one very much out of keeping with the Church's desire—at least in recent centuries—to separate itself from politics. The Church O'Connor knew and loved was a slow church, one committed to its ancient principles and practice, one that was resistant to change—and even if and when change was deemed necessary, its movement was glacial in speed.

This is the ethos of the Church O'Connor grew up with and recommitted herself to. It informed her perceptions of contemporary politics, and it informed her vision as a fiction writer as well. It seems almost inevitable that her stories feature a clash between her deep theological vision, informed by that ethos and by the history of the Church, and the lesser vision (to her mind) manifest in popular politics. In such a contest of worldviews, as dramatized in her stories, the latter would not stand a chance.

## The Idolatry of Racism

Whereas the Church's slowness was regarded as a virtue by O'Connor, for many Catholics—especially black Catholics—it was and continues to be a source of frustration. In his groundbreaking study *Racial Justice and the Catholic Church*, African American priest and scholar Bryan N. Massingale offers a frank look at the contemporary Catholic Church and demonstrates the ways in which, despite its attempts to embrace African Americans, it remains blinded by its whiteness well into the twenty-first century. The American Catholic Church, on the whole, is still governed by a mostly white hierarchy (i.e., bishops and cardinals descended from white Europeans) and lacks black representation among priests, sisters, deacons, lay pastoral ministers, and educators; it still privileges white forms of worship (European music and contemporary folk music, for instance) over black forms (African music, jazz or gospel); and it still images Christ, the Virgin Mary, and God the Father as white, despite the historical fact that Jesus and Mary were Middle Eastern people of color and despite the fact that the appearance of God, as an act of imagination, ought to incorporate the many nonwhite varieties of human beings, all of whom are made in the image and likeness of God. In addition, the Church is still practically segregated, if not officially so, with most whites choosing to belong to majority white parishes, leaving blacks to their own often impoverished parishes. Despite the steady "browning" of America and American Catholics, thanks to the many Latino/a immigrants absorbed by the United States, the Church continues to conduct itself as a white Church and remains stubbornly unconsciousness of that whiteness. Again, in keeping with critical whiteness theory, whiteness constitutes an emptiness or absence and, therefore, is a condition often unperceived. When it is seen, it is regarded as the norm, making nonwhite peoples deviants from that norm. Whiteness becomes the standard by which everything is measured. As a result, African Americans are regarded as visitors in their own Church, rather than full-fledged members with the right to claim ownership of it.

Clearly, the racism that has afflicted and shaped the culture of the United States has similarly afflicted and shaped the culture of the Church. Both Massingale and African American scholar M. Shawn Copeland have called out this persistent racial injustice based in an implicit assertion of white supremacy, going so far as to speak of racism by going beyond the traditionally cited "ethical categories of structural sin or intrinsic evil" and identifying it as a form of "idolatry" (Massingale, "Has the Silence Been Broken?" 151). In her challenging theological study of the treatment of black women's bodies throughout the history of America and of the Church, *Enfleshing Freedom*, Copeland states boldly, "Racism spoils the spirit and insults the holy; it is idolatry. Racism coerces religion's transcendent orientation to surrender the absolute to what is finite, empirical and arbitrary, and contradicts the very nature of religion. Racism displaces the Transcendent Other and selects and enthrones its own deity" (109–10).

Similarly, Massingale argues that "U.S. and global Catholicism have been co-opted into an idolatrous belief system that practically maintains that the sacred and the holy can be definitively mediated and unambiguously encountered only through white cultural products" ("white" music, "white" artistic representations of divinity and holiness), and that this represents a "complicity in racial superiority" and constitutes "the essence of a compromised idolatrous identity" ("Has the Silence Been Broken?" 151).

This metaphor of racism—particularly the institutional racism manifest in the Catholic Church—as a form of "idolatry," a belief system that displaces and supplants the truths that Christians and Catholics are supposed to believe in, offers yet another perspective on the faith O'Connor practiced and the Church she belonged to. Just as O'Connor was sometimes blinded to the white privilege she enjoyed socially and politically, she was blinded by the white privilege granted her by her Church. In choosing to ally herself with the world view of the pre–Vatican II Church, rooted in the Old World and largely untouched by the participation of people of color, as opposed to the newly emerging Church in its efforts (limited as they were) to reinvent itself in the context of the New World of diversity and modernity—efforts which would include the attempt, at least, to welcome African Americans and people of color into full participation—was O'Connor choosing to keep faith with an idol, rather than the actual Church, whose liberal views she found distasteful? Is it possible to see her preference for and fidelity to that Church, founded as it was on principles of white supremacy, as an unconscious and, thus, unintentional endorsement of those principles? Granted, it is impossible to read the human heart, and we have no way of knowing with any certainty what O'Connor believed concerning the issue of equality between the races. But the combination of her origin and immersion in an overtly racist society and her spiritual and cultural grounding in a covertly racist Church would have made it practically impossible to escape being shaped by those forces in ways both hidden and plain. To return to an earlier metaphor, the theological and spiritual lenses through which she looks at the world in order to create her fiction are clouded, rather than clear, her vision partial rather than full, and, therefore, limited. As we have seen,

O'Connor again and again acknowledged such limitations. "The poet is traditionally a blind man," she once remarked, recalling the tradition associated with the ancient bards, including Homer and the singer of Beowulf, "but the Christian poet, and storyteller as well, is like the blind man whom Christ touched, who looked then and saw men as if they were trees, but walking" (*MM* 184). O'Connor identifies the blind man's sudden epiphany as "the beginning of vision" and "an invitation to deeper and stranger visions that we shall have to learn to accept if we want to realize a truly Christian literature" (*MM* 184). This "deeper and stranger" vision is what O'Connor strove for, and as the power of her stories would suggest, she achieves that vision quite often. But no artist can see everything, and sometimes it is as instructive for us as readers to observe what is absent in a work of art as it is to observe what is present. Perhaps in reading O'Connor's fiction we might become as perceptive and discerning as George, the African American character who appears in "The Barber," who in listening to the talk of the white men in the shop "can hear what he hears and can hear two times that much." Listening in this way might enable us to hear what O'Connor doesn't say as well as what she does (*CS* 24).

## Race and Revelation

In 1964, a few months before her death and after an extended dry spell during which she began to worry that she was incapable of writing any new fiction, Flannery O'Connor wrote one of her finest and most celebrated stories. "Revelation" tells the story of Ruby Turpin, a deeply Christian woman who has lost sight of the foundational basis of her faith—Christ's exhortation to "Love one another" (John 13:34)—and has adopted instead an idolatrous belief in a racist ethos that rests on the superiority of white people over black. Mrs. Turpin is at heart a decent woman who has been misshapen by a culture that runs counter to her faith. At night her better angel signals to her the spiritual peril she is in. As she falls asleep, "naming the classes of people," placing most black people at the bottom, the "white trash" beside them, and the rest in ascending order according to their wealth and property, she is perturbed by the failure of her vision to judge people justly, to identify who they truly are and where they truly belong; by the time sleep arrives, "all the classes of people were moiling and roiling around in her head, and she would dream they were all crammed in together in a box car, being ridden off to be put in a gas oven" (*CS* 492). In her dreams, Ruby senses what her conscious mind denies in the daylight, her own complicity in evil.

Mrs. Turpin's life is changed forever one day when she is in the doctor's office, waiting to be seen. It is her husband's physical illness, rather than her psychic and spiritual one, that brings her there; nonetheless, it will prove the site where she begins to heal. When she is struck in the eye by a book hurled at her by a young woman named Mary Grace, a Wellesley College student who is enraged by Mrs. Turpin's racist talk, she is made painfully aware of her sinfulness. As the girl physically attacks Mrs. Turpin, Ruby wrestles with her and extracts from her the message the girl wants to convey—that she is a "wart hog" from "hell," the place of her origin and the place of her destiny (*CS* 500). Ruby is astonished by this ugly accusation, which breaks into her settled life with a terrible violence, robbing her of her certainty and her peace, and spends much of the rest of the story trying to deny it. Ruby engages in two more wrestling matches after the initial one with Mary Grace: First she wrestles with herself, trying to eradicate the image Mary Grace has introduced into her imagination, and then she engages in a wrestling match with God, demanding to know, at last, who he thinks he is to send her such a message. Ruby, whom O'Connor refers to as "a country female Jacob" in one of her letters (*HB* 577), wrestles with no mere angel but the Creator of the universe himself until she extracts a blessing: a vision of the Kingdom of God, one wherein Christ's beatitudes prove true, as those first in this life (she and Claude) are last in the procession of saints and those last in this life (including the black people she despises) are first. She takes the Kingdom of Heaven by violence and makes it hers. In the end, "Revelation" is the story of a good woman whose mind and heart are tainted by the legacy of racial oppression she inherits but is saved, ultimately, by a truer vision that supplants her flawed and fraught one. "Revelation" is also, in many ways, a story about Flannery O'Connor. In creating Ruby Turpin, O'Connor has inadvertently invented a version of herself, a kind of double, who undergoes a conversion experience that echoes and maps her own struggle against the social and historical forces that have shaped her thinking and beliefs about race.

On first reading, this may seem an unlikely equivalence. The differences that separate Ruby Turpin from O'Connor are more apparent than any similarities they might share. In her letters, O'Connor refers to Ruby repeatedly as "a country woman" (*HB* 546, 569, 577), a person who does not share the cultivation, education, and enlarged perspective of a person like O'Connor. She is a small-minded woman, severely limited by the circumscribed life she leads. And yet, in a letter she writes to her friend, Cecil Dawkins, when she is in the midst of writing the story, O'Connor confesses, "I've set all . . . aside and am working on a story that I like and am at the moment right enthusiastic about. It has one of those country women in it who just sort of springs to life; you can't hold them down or shut their mouths" (*HB* 546). The character of Mrs. Turpin comes easily to O'Connor, perhaps, in part, because she is a familiar type, the sort of person O'Connor has met often in middle Georgia, including, as she writes in letter to Elizabeth Hester on March 14, 1964, in the hospital she stays in recuperating from surgery (*HB* 569). But there is another kind of familiarity at play here. There is something in Ruby Turpin that delights O'Connor and reminds her of herself. For all the crudeness of her racism, Ruby is a woman who spends much of her life observing people, trying to see and understand them. She goes about this in all the wrong ways, of course, but who of us doesn't? We may use different criteria for judging people—perhaps instead of the kinds of shoes people wear, we might use the way people speak as a means of categorizing and defining them—but the fact is we are engaging in the same human activity Ruby Turpin is. And no one pursues this activity of close and critical observation of one's fellow human beings with more verve and dedication than a fiction writer. As Ruby casts her eye around the room, she creates a narrative for each of the people she observes, imagining their lives based on their appearance, and divining motives for their behavior—the "lean stringy old fellow" who keeps his eyes closed "so as not to get up and offer her a seat," the "well-dressed, gray-haired lady" whose eyes convey a message of solidarity with regard to the dirty child who is taking up too much room on the sofa: "if that child belonged to me, he would have some manners and move over" (*CS* 488). Ruby is practicing the habits of a fiction writer—the very habits O'Connor is engaging in as she creates the story—and, thus, channels her creator, albeit in a comic, cartoonish way. In a sense, at the least at the start of the story, Flannery and Ruby are co-creators of Mrs. Turpin's tale.

This potential identity between the two women, one fictional and one actual, produces some fascinating and uncomfortable dynamics as the story unfolds. As Mrs. Turpin observes the "white trash" woman, focusing on her "gritty looking" clothes, her snuff-stained lips, and the "little piece of red paper ribbon" that ties "her dirty yellow hair," she mentally pronounces, "Worse than niggers any day" (*CS* 490). O'Connor is, of course, channeling what a woman like Mrs. Turpin would think, rather than her own thoughts; however, in a sense, since Mrs. Turpin exists only as a creation of O'Connor's imagination, these *are* her own thoughts. They are the kinds of judgments that would almost inevitably occur to white people living in the rural South born and bred in a culture that conditions them to hold black people in contempt. One's proximity to the category of "nigger," the word assigned by a racist caste system to the lowest instantiation of humanity, is the measure of one's worth. This is a language learned young, and it is a language O'Connor and Mrs. Turpin share. Thus, Ruby becomes a shadow version of Flannery, a dark projection of the internal racist self that O'Connor externalizes and chastens.

The agent of that chastening, Mary Grace, is also a shadow figure of an actual person, O'Connor's friend and correspondent Maryat Lee. O'Connor acknowledges as much in several of her letters, but even without this admission, the identity shared by the two women would be clear. In addition to their shared names, Mary Grace and Maryat Lee share an alma mater (Wellesley College), a strong sense of identification with northern liberal values when it comes to matters of race, and a powerful aversion to the racist attitudes so prevalent in her native Southland. In her letters, O'Connor admits to an equal admiration for both of her characters: "I like Mrs. Turpin as well as Mary Grace," she writes to Maryat Lee (*HB* 577), and in a letter to Elizabeth Hester she admits to loving Mary Grace because she is a version of her beloved friend: "Maryat's niece asked her why I had made Mary Grace so ugly. 'Because Flannery loves her,' said Maryat. Very perceptive girl" (*HB* 578). It is clear that the kinship Flannery and Maryat share in life (both despite and because of their differences) is echoed in the kinship shared by Ruby and Mary Grace. Even before Mary Grace throws the book at Mrs. Turpin, the latter is disturbed by the accusatorial gaze the young woman trains on her: "She was looking at her as if she had known and disliked her all her life—all of Mrs. Turpin's life, it seemed too, not just all the girl's life. Why, girl, I don't even know you, Mrs. Turpin said silently" (*CS* 495). After she is struck, Mrs. Turpin is forced to retract this denial as she looks into the fierce, brilliant eyes of her nemesis/familiar: "There was no doubt in her mind that the girl did know her, knew her in some intense and personal way, beyond time and place and condition" (*CS* 500). Both sets of women share an intense intimacy of the kind shareable only by two people who occupy opposite ends of a spectrum of thought and belief, wherein each possesses knowledge of the other as an inverse version of herself. Clearly, the *agon* based on their divergent ideas about race that Mrs. Turpin and Mary Grace act out in the doctor's office is an extreme version of the friendly one carried on between O'Connor and Maryat Lee in their correspondence. It is part of the grace of their friendship that Flannery and Maryat are able to disagree amicably about such potentially volatile issues. O'Connor hints at this in a letter she writes to her friend just a few weeks before her death after seeing a photo of Maryat as a child: "That child in that picture is you all right. I'd have knowed you right off. . . . It's fortunate we didn't get together at that age. We would have blown something up. I would have found the matches and let you light the fuse" (*HB* 584). This is, in some ways, an apt description of the conflict O'Connor portrays between Ruby Turpin and Mary Grace, with Mrs. Turpin providing the flammable material and Mary Grace setting it on fire.

Given this doubling, and given the centrality and salvific consequences of the conflict between Mrs. Turpin and Mary Grace, the story conveys something of the pattern of O'Connor's own gradual and constant conversion toward an understanding of the mystery of race. One of the unexpected consequences of her run in with Mary Grace is Mrs. Turpin's emerging awareness of the personhood of African Americans. Early in the story, she speaks of black people only in insulting terms, though she does make one allowance (noted in Chapter 2), granting that if God had decided to make her black, she would be a "neat clean respectable Negro woman" as opposed to a "nigger" (*CS* 491). The one black person who appears early in the story is a delivery boy who enters the doctor's office in search of the secretary. Mrs. Turpin helpfully instructs the boy, who has presumably made many such deliveries, "You see that button here, boy? ... You can punch that and she'll come. She's probably in the back somewhere" (*CS* 495). "'Is thas right?' the boy said agreeably, as if he had never seen the button before," responding as he must according to the racial code that insists that white people be treated deferentially, no matter how idiotic their behavior might be. Mrs. Turpin seems unaware of the playacting the boy engages in, though the narrator is not: "She sometime out," he says, referring to the secretary, after pushing the buzzer, "and twisted around to face his audience, his elbows behind him on the counter" (*CS* 495). The boy is careful to play his part before the watchful gaze of a roomful of white people. The requisite black person's pantomime is a performance that would be visible to them as such only in the breach rather than the observance.

Later in the story, this circumstance changes. After Mrs. Turpin is struck in the face by Mary Grace's book, her interaction with black people is more nuanced and knowing. When she greets the field hands returning from their day of work with a bucket of ice water, as is her habit, she invites them into a rare communion with her, telling the story of what happened in the doctor's office. Their response, in keeping with the delivery boy's, is deferential, saying the things white people typically expect to hear, assuring Mrs. Turpin she is "sweet" (she's not) and "pretty" (she's not) and "stout" (a truth at last) (*CS* 505). But Ruby is atypically alert to the dramatic dynamics of the conversation, recognizing "Negro flattery" when she hears it and dismissing it as false and meaningless. In a further attempt at intimacy, an attempt to break through the barrier imposed by the code that forbids meaningful communication between the races, she relays the terrible message Mary Grace delivered—a message she has shared with no other human being, not even her husband, Claud. Instead of the felt compassion and human sympathy she craves, the black women continue with the performance required by the code, a theatrical spectacle of feigned outrage and excessive reassurances of her virtues, all culminating in the pronouncement, "Jesus satisfied with her!" (CS 505). In her rage, disappointment, and increased sense of isolation, Mrs. Turpin responds inwardly and defensively: "Idiots! . . . You could never say anything intelligent to a nigger. You could talk at them but not with them" (CS 505). This passage may suggest that Mrs. Turpin is fooled by the mask of witlessness the field hands don, but it also simultaneously suggests a growing awareness of the complex dynamics at work in black/white communication. The division she notes is a source of sadness to her, the fact that the races talk *at* each other rather than *with* each other, and it impoverishes the people on both sides. Even so, she continues to reify that divide by using the word, "nigger," continuing the old habit of objectifying the very human beings she seeks communion with.

The final movement in Mrs. Turpin's journey toward an understanding of the mystery of race occurs, of course, when she receives the vision of the heavenly procession at the conclusion of the story. Walking across the fields toward the hogs she must hose down and feed, as she does every evening, "She had the look of a woman going single-handed, weaponless, into battle" (CS 505). In the light of the setting sun—an image wherein O'Connor invokes the identity between the sun and the Son, as she does in other stories—she asks God a question and demands an answer, "How am I a hog and me both?" (CS 506). Ruby's view has been too schematic, as the implosion of her faulty system ranking class and race would suggest, too black and white. One is either good or evil, saved or damned, a sinner or a saint—her theology makes no allowances for human complexity, the role of saving grace, and the need for God's mercy. Her soliloquy culminates in a final surge of fury that shakes her as she roars, "Who do you think you are?" (CS 507).

The response Ruby receives is threefold. First, she sees Claud's truck, tiny in the distance, making its way across the highway, and receives a vision of the tentative and contingent nature of life: "It looked like a child's toy. At any moment a bigger truck might smash into it and scatter Claud's and the niggers' brains all over the road" (CS 508). The fact of whose brains are whose, those of a white farmer or those of "his" black workers, does not signify. In the face of death, all are the equal, despite Ruby's use of the pejorative term racist habit has inculcated in her. A second vision then comes to Ruby, a glimpse of the mystery of the world she inhabits, one that is suffused with divine presence. Even the pigs in the pen before her "pant with a secret life." Mrs. Turpin, large as she is, realizes how small and vulnerable the individual human person is, how dependent upon God all creatures, human and animal, are. And then, in one final, fantastic, visionary moment, she sees the heavenly procession of the Communion of Saints:

> She saw the streak [in the sky] as a vast swinging bridge extending upward form the earth through a field of living fire. Upon it a vast horde of souls were rumbling toward heaven. There were whole companies of white-trash, clean for the first time in their lives, and bands of black niggers in white robes, and battalions of freaks and lunatics shouting and clapping and leaping like frogs. And bringing up the end of the procession was a tribe of people whom she recognized at once as those who, like herself and Claud, had always had a little of everything and the God-given wit to use it right. She learned forward to observe them closer. They were marching behind the others with great dignity, accountable as they had always been for good order and common sense and respectable behavior. They alone were on key. Yet she could see by their shocked and altered faces that even their virtues were being burned away. (CS 508)

The vision Ruby receives is a clear corrective to the coarse classification system she had lived by, to her bigoted view of blacks, as well as of poor whites, the disabled, the insane, and all other human beings she thought were beneath her. The sinned-against, the marginalized, and the dispossessed are much beloved of God and received first into the kingdom, while the self-righteous and supposedly virtuous bring up the rear. The good news is there is a place for them in the kingdom; the bad news, for Ruby, is that the place is not nearly as privileged as she had imagined.

Although O'Connor's journey toward a fuller understanding of race is not as extreme as Mrs. Turpin's—many of the things Ruby needs to learn, Flannery is well aware of—their journeys and the destinations they arrive at are similar in kind. The threefold vision Mrs. Turpin wrests from God is a corollary to the incarnational, analogical, anagogic vision O'Connor cultivates in the writing of her fiction—a vision O'Connor has been wresting from God every day for much of her life, from her earliest days as a writer at Iowa (as evidenced in her journal) through to her conception and execution of "Revelation," one of her last and best stories. "Revelation" is, in some ways, an allegory of her own slow conversion. In a letter to Elizabeth Hester, O'Connor once wrote, "I don't know if anybody can be converted without seeing themselves in a kind of blasting annihilating light, a blast that will last a lifetime" (*HB* 427). In another letter to Hester written a few weeks later, she would continue in this vein: "I don't think of conversion as being once and for all and that's that. I think once the process is begun and continues that you are continually turning inward toward God and away from your own egocentricity and that you have to see this selfish side of yourself in order to turn away from it" (*HB* 430). Through the agency of Mary Grace, Ruby Turpin discovers the warthog in herself and understands her need for forgiveness and redemption. This saving self-recognition may not be evident in the letters O'Connor exchanges with Maryat Lee—she is too busy enjoying playing her quasi-racist role for that—but her recognition of the important role her friend and worthy opponent has played in her life is clear in the story. O'Connor's conversion to a full understanding and acceptance of racial equality is by no means complete. She is still, from time to time, unaware of the ways in which her whiteness prevents her from seeing fully and clearly. One such example occurs even in this story, wherein the African Americans in the procession are described as "black niggers in white robes." As Timothy Caron points out, the description of Ruby's vision, even in the midst of her epiphany, is "still freighted with the offensively racist language of the white South." The word may arise more from Ruby's consciousness than the narrator's, but its presence suggests that both writer and character have a way to go in terms of their conversion with regard to race. In addition, the juxtaposition of colors imply that the "blackness" of African Americans can be redeemed only by "whiteness," a color they can put on but can never fully own. This, in combination with the antics and capering of the so-called freaks and lunatics—and perhaps even the black souls, as well, depending upon how one reads the syntax of the third sentence describing the vision—suggests that "this is not a procession of equals ascending toward heaven" (155). What this story dramatizes is O'Connor's attempt to escape the burden of a white culture, a white church, and what is in some ways a white theology. It should come as no surprise that she does not entirely break free. As O'Connor attests in her letters, conversion is never finished. Like the blind man who is touched by Christ and sees men who look like trees, it is only the beginning of vision.

# 4 / "Africanist Presence" and the Role of Black Bodies

While it is illuminating to consider Flannery O'Connor's views on race in light of the sociological, political, historical, and theological contexts she lived and worked in the midst of, it is equally essential to consider the literary context her writing emerges from and participates in, particularly with regard to the treatment of race. Examining O'Connor's work through a theoretical lens that focuses on the ways in which American authors write about race enables readers to see more clearly the unique contributions and challenges presented by O'Connor's fiction. It also reminds us of the fact that race has long been a preoccupation of American literature, both conscious and unconscious, and that O'Connor is far from alone in taking on the difficult task of writing about black people from the limited perspective of a white consciousness. As might be predicted, given her grounding in Catholic theology and her analogical imagination, her approach proves to be characteristically concerned with incarnation, the physical reality of what it means to be embodied as black and white.

In her study of race in American literature, *Playing in the Dark: Whiteness and the Literary Imagination*, Toni Morrison calls for a reevaluation of the American literary canon, paying particular attention to the pervasive element she terms "American Africanism." Her book is meant to serve as a kind of model for the "investigation into the ways in which a nonwhite Africanlike (or Africanist) presence or persona was constructed in the United States, and the imaginative uses this fabricated presence served" (6). Morrison focuses her analysis on a handful of canonical white authors (mostly male), including Melville, Poe, Faulkner, and Hemingway, though she does make note of O'Connor twice, once with reference to "The Artificial Nigger" and once in lamenting the fact that literary critics have not paid sufficient attention to the Africanist presence in American fiction in general and in O'Connor's fiction in particular: "They see no connection between God's grace and Africanist 'othering' in Flannery O'Connor" (14).

Morrison's critique seemed to arrive at a propitious time in many ways when it was published in 1992, as the American literary canon was being interrogated by critics and readers and as her own literary contributions were reshaping American literature. In the decades since Morrison issued her challenge and in response to her call, critics have made up for their relative silence on these matters, as evidenced by the many thoughtful studies of O'Connor's treatment of her black characters that I have identified earlier in this book, some of which were actually published before *Playing in the Dark* made its debut. While these critical explorations have helped to elucidate the ways in which black characters function in her fiction, it seems that given O'Connor's Catholicism, the role that her faith plays in the theological vision informing her art, and the centrality of the trope of Incarnation in both, attention to the *bodies* of O'Connor's black characters and their place in the larger Mystical *Body* of Christ might prove helpful in understanding the nature of the Africanist presence in her fiction.

Such an approach raises some fascinating questions: How are black bodies imaged in the stories? What does the black body signify to O'Connor and what might it signify to the reader? What does blackness mean to someone with an analogical imagination, an imagination that perceives the ways in which physical reality speaks to and of human life in the Divine? Although we may not be able to arrive at definitive answers to these questions, a close look at representative stories in light of Morrison's reenvisioning and O'Connor's Catholic perspective opens up some provocative possibilities.

In her opening argument for her book, Morrison suggests that Americans have long labored under the delusion that the United States is the product of white male minds. Similarly, there was, for a long time, a tacit agreement that American literature consisted almost entirely of white male visionaries. Morrison challenges this white blindness, asserting that the four-hundred-year-old presence of Africans and African Americans has "shaped the body politic, the Constitution, and the entire history of the culture" and has played a significant role in the development of that culture's literature (5). Indeed, contemplation of "the overwhelming presence of black people in the United States" is central to any understanding of our history and our national literature (5). Morrison's argument holds true for O'Connor's fiction, as well. Though it would seem that white people and white people's lives are the main focus of her fiction (as discussed earlier), their stories are told against the sometimes visible, sometimes invisible, but always abiding presence of African Americans. Though it has been suggested that these characters perform minor or secondary roles (as stereotypes, as catalysts, as cyphers with no perceivable interior life), when we look closely at the stories, every black character signifies, in some way, and signifies differently. At least part of that difference is attributable to and discernable through representations of the physical presence of each character, young and old, male and female, dark-skinned and light. An examination of a select few of the Africanists that appear in her fiction will demonstrate O'Connor's careful attention to the body and reveal something of her thoughts about the power and limitation of embodiment, both those consciously and unconsciously expressed.

## A Personal Perspective and a Physical Perspective

The body, and the female body in particular, was of considerable interest to O'Connor, in terms of both her personal life and her vocation. The watershed experience of her life was the diagnosis of lupus she was given when she was twenty-five years old. At a time when most people are enjoying the robust health that comes with youth, O'Connor had to endure the debilitating symptoms of what she jokingly called her "DREAD DISEASE" in a letter to Maryat Lee (*HB* 266; emphasis O'Connor's). For the remainder of her life, from December 1949 until her death in August 1964, she would be subject to its severe demands and its heartbreaking frailties. Lupus is a brutal disease, an autoimmune disorder in which the body attacks its own tissues, including joints, major organs, and the central nervous system. It is wildly unpredictable as it manifests differently in every patient. Flannery's lupus would not look like her father's (which she had witnessed close up as his health deteriorated); it would prove much more virulent and incapacitating. She would suffer dangerously high fevers and rampant infections, necrosis of the jaw, which would make eating an ordeal, and deterioration of her joints, hipbone, and skeletal muscles—so much so that she would need to use a walker and crutches, which she playfully referred to as her "flying buttresses," to move about (*HB* 151). To worsen matters, O'Connor's physical deterioration was aided and abetted by the drugs she was given to control the lupus. Her daily high-dosage injections of the corticosteroid ACTH (injections she would learn to administer herself) would provide some temporary relief of her symptoms, but they weakened her bones, thinned her hair, and caused swelling, creating a "moon-face" effect that embarrassed her. In most of the photographs taken of O'Connor after her diagnosis, she appears aged beyond her years and bears little resemblance to the attractive young woman who went off to Iowa just a few years before the onset of the disease.

But O'Connor was a fighter, famously so. In her letters, she describes with patience, wit, and good humor the gradual diminishment of her physical capacities. Not only would she learn to live with her disease, but she would also learn to find grace in it and regard it as a divine gift. In a letter to Elizabeth Hester written in 1956, she writes: "I have never been anywhere but sick. In a sense, sickness is a place, more instructive than a long trip to Europe, and it's always a place where there's no company; where nobody can follow. Sickness before death is a very appropriate thing and I think those who don't have it miss one of God's mercies" (*HB* 163). At the age when most young people are still laboring under the delusion that they are immortal, O'Connor looked her mortality in the face every day, and this gave her strength and purpose. She knew she had no time to waste. Despite the daily assault on her body, she poured herself into her writing, refusing to give up her vocation regardless of the precious energy it cost her. Given her daily struggle with an intractable illness that altered her body and her way of being in the world, it seems perfectly natural that her fiction should be filled with characters who suffer physical, mental, and spiritual limitations—missing limbs, deformity, mental impairment, obesity, deafness, muteness, bad eyes, and weak hearts—and that these afflictions often lead to their salvation. This, of course, is classic Catholic Christian theology, only O'Connor was not merely *writing* about the cross, the pattern of suffering that leads to redemption—she was living it.

O'Connor's bodily suffering instilled in her a bone-deep knowing of the trials the human body can and does endure, and it drove her to seek a theological understanding of embodiment and its meaning. Some of that meaning she pursues in the ways we might expect a religiously inclined person to seek it—through prayer, spiritual direction, and the reading and study of sacred and theological texts. But she also sought meaning in the way that artists do—through her craft. Thus, the body figures prominently in O'Connor's fiction as she explores and interrogates the ways in which our physical qualities—those that might be counted as blessings as well as those regarded as limitations and afflictions—determine who we are and who we become.

## Body, Race, and Being: A Catholic Perspective

In her study *Enfleshing Freedom: Body, Race, & Being*, M. Shawn Copeland explores the historical perception and treatment of black women's bodies in light of Catholic theology. Beginning with Genesis and the story of the creation, Copeland reviews the Judeo-Christian concept of *Imago Dei*, which holds the human body as sacred since it is made in the image and likeness of God. Our bodies relate us back to the source of our being, the creator, and they also connect us to all other created beings. By virtue of the body we belong to God, to ourselves, and to one another. Copeland further reminds us of the fact that, as embodied creatures, the body constitutes the ground of our being. It is the means through which we know and experience the world. Its function and meaning for us, at its most basic level and in its most immediate sense, is physical in nature. However, the body is not merely adjunctive to us, something that is *with* us—it *is* us, in some deep and abiding way (7). It is impossible for us to abstract ourselves from our bodily immersion in the physical world—the eyes we see through, the hands we touch with, the brain we think with, all color and shape our experience of the world and help determine our identities.

This is true of all bodies, Copeland argues, and it is true of black bodies: "To speak in this way is to recognize that the black body is a site of divine revelation and, thus, is a basic human sacrament" (24). However, our encounter with black bodies, as Americans, and with female black bodies, in particular, "has been shaped, although not determined, by the historical matrix of slavery" (25). Drawing on historical sources and narratives of emancipated black women, Copeland chronicles in brutal detail the ways in which slavery perpetrated violence on women's bodies, from their first capture in their native land, to the horror of the middle passage, through the unnatural lives they were forced to lead, characterized by back-breaking labor, sexual violence, forced reproduction, and the denial of their rights as mothers to their own children. This latter abuse is a particular violence that marked the lives of enslaved black women, "who bore life only to surrender their children to the maw of the plantation, to an order and culture of death" (34). Morrison, in *Playing in the Dark*, also comments on this phenomenon as a key feature of the inherited perception of African American women. As a result of being taken from their own mothers, as well as suffering the loss of their children, "slave women are 'natally dead,' with no obligations to their offspring or their own parents" (21). This, historically, created a circumstance in which black women, insofar as they had any maternal instincts, were required to direct their attentions to the needs of white children in the families they were owned by. Thus, they would become nannies and mammies, "black bodies" that served as substitutes for the white mothers who had given birth to the children, as well as serving as sexual surrogates (as was so often the case) for their white mistresses as they endured the outrage of rape by their masters and the indignity of having to give birth to the illegitimate children that resulted from this sexual violence (26). These are just few of the ways in which the black body, theoretically a human sacrament, is defaced and desecrated by slavery, and that violation has continued long after the replacement of the official institution of slavery with the unofficial institution of racism: "An intrinsic evil, racism is lethal to bodies, to black bodies, to the body of Christ, to Eucharist" (Copeland 109).

The body possessed by a black woman is, thus, defined not only by its evident physical characteristics. It is also inscribed by history. Cultural anthropologist Mary Douglas, whose work Copeland cites in her study, calls attention to the body's function as a code or image for social reality when she speaks of "social bodies": "The social body constrains the way the physical body is perceived" and is dependent upon the meaning and significance assigned to race, gender, sexuality, and physical traits. This meaning ascribed to human bodies on the basis of these demarcating qualities, in turn, "influences, perhaps even determines, the trajectories of concrete human lives" (Douglas 73). Copeland's study, among other ideas, considers the relation between the social body and the physical body with regard to the lives of black women in the United States—lives that continue to be shaped by the consequences of slavery, economic injustice, the curse of Jim Crow, the threat of violence, and the pervasive conditions of racism and antifeminism.

## Motherhood in Black and White: "Everything That Rises Must Converge"

O'Connor once wrote, in her dismissal of Eudora Welty's story written in outraged response to the assassination of civil rights activist Medgar Evers discussed in Chapter 2, "the topical is poison." She goes on in that letter, however, to qualify that blanket statement: "I got away with it in 'Everything That Rises' but only because I say a plague on everybody's house as far as the race business goes" (*HB* 537). O'Connor's story, in fact, is among her most provocative. A middle-aged white woman and her grown son, Julian, board a city bus one evening en route to her exercise class. She has high blood pressure and needs to lose weight, and Julian must accompany her because she fears riding the bus alone since the enforcement of integration. Julian, who can barely countenance his mother's blatantly racist and reactionary attitudes, thinks himself a liberal and an integrationist, though O'Connor's probing into his consciousness demonstrates quite plainly that Julian does not really believe in the equality of the races. He is a poser, an impudent and overgrown child who wears the guise of liberal politics as he sticks pins in his mother's ideological balloon of white superiority. Into this scene of child/parent dysfunction steps another mother and son, who could not be more different from Julian and his mother in outward appearance, but who we gradually come to recognize as a shadow version of the pair. Sitting, ensconced in his "mental bubble" imagining ways to ingratiate himself with "negroes" and thereby outrage his mother, "he was tilted out of his fantasy ... as the bus stopped. The door opened and with a sucking hiss and out of the dark a large, gaily dressed, sullen-looking colored woman got on with a little boy" (CS 415).

Given his role as the center of consciousness in the story, the reader sees the events unfold mostly through Julian's eyes. The observations made about the characters are his observations, and he immediately goes about studying this black woman, describing her physical body, but also implying a recognition of her social body:

> She was a giant of a woman. Her face was set not only to meet opposition but to seek it out. The downward tilt of her large lower lip was like a warning sign: DON'T TAMPER WITH ME. Her bulging figure was encased in a green crepe dress and her feet overflowed in red shoes. She had on a hideous hat. A purple velvet flap came down on one side of it and stood up on the other; the rest of it was green and looked like a cushion with the stuffing out. She carried a mammoth red pocketbook that bulged throughout as if it were stuffed with rocks. (CS 415)

As is typical of O'Connor's breathtaking economy, everything we need to know about this woman for the purposes of the plot is evident in the description, as is the arc of the entire story, from the "hideous" hat, that is an exact replica of the one Julian's mother is wearing, thereby marking the woman as her "black double "(CS 419) and setting up the inevitable conflict between the two, to the red purse seemingly full of rocks with which the woman will eventually strike Julian's mother, precipitating her death and his awakening to his culpability in his own mother's demise. Julian describes the woman as a "giant," attributing to her a kind of mythic stature and also implying that she, like most giants in most tales, is a bully. Julian's own mother, by contrast, is consistently characterized as being diminutive (if a bit overweight) and vulnerable. In contrast to the black woman's ungainly feet that can't be contained by her shoes, Julian's mother's "feet in little pumps dangled like a child's that did not quite reach the floor" (CS 414). The barely suppressed rage Julian sees in her protruding lower lip marks her as a type, the archetypal Angry Black Woman upon whom much violence has been inflicted and who is just waiting for a worthy object to unleash her righteous rage upon. This is further confirmed as the woman sits beside Julian, seething as (we assume) she notices the similarity between her hat and that of the supercilious white woman across the aisle. She is not amused. Julian concentrates his attention on the woman, describing her through a series of similes and metaphors as "an angry cat," "a monkey," "a volcano about to become active," and, finally, after she explodes with rage at the end of the story, "a piece of machinery that had been given one ounce of pressure too much" (CS 416–18). It is notable that Julian describes the woman's identity mostly in terms of animals, forces of nature, and machinery, as if she were not fully human. In the rare moments when he highlights her in human terms, he sees her as very physical and very female, noting "the mammoth bosom" and "the red pocketbook upright on the bulging green thighs," terms that emphasize her gender, her sexuality, and her maternal qualities. This is another archetype commonly occurring in white characterizations of black women—the combination of sexuality and maternity—also evident in O'Connor's characterization of the large black woman who appears in "The Artificial Nigger." In one of her letters, O'Connor refers to the latter as "a black mountain of maternity" (HB 78) who also arouses both filial and sexual longing in young Nelson, who has never seen a black woman before. In addition, later on as Julian castigates his mother for trying to give the woman's little boy a penny and thereby brings retribution upon herself, he describes the black woman as "an uppity Negro" (though he avers she is more than that) and "the whole colored race" which has risen up to punish his mother for a lifetime of racist crimes (CS 419). His perception of her social body trumps any perception of her actual body, preventing Julian from any human connection with the woman. Far from being a "human sacrament," her body is an affront, a violent reminder of a racist past and present, and, therefore, a source of physical and psychic pain to white people. The only moment that suggests even a modicum of sympathy in the story appears when he describes her standing before him, "her shoulders lifted and her face frozen with frustrated rage" (418). Since we never get access to the woman's consciousness in the story, we cannot know the particular source of her rage any more than Julian can, so, granted, our compassion is minimal. However, as inheritors of a culture based on violence against African Americans, we can guess the outrage that begets her outrage.

It is not clear how much control O'Connor has—or can have—over the dynamics of the story. In her letter in which she suggests that she "got away with" her topical story focused on integration because she said "a plague on everybody's house," she implies that there is equal blame to go around for the violence that has unfolded during the fight for civil rights, both on her imagined bus and on the real buses. Granted, it is likely true that O'Connor is making a theological point here, as D. Dean Shackleford, among others, notes in his essay devoted to "the black outsider" in O'Connor's fiction, "Original sin and its results are a part of human nature, regardless of race" (85), and that O'Connor's suggestion of the flawed nature shared by all the characters implies belief in equality of all in God's eyes. However, the contemporary reader who has borne witness to the upheaval of the civil rights movement, to the crimes perpetrated against peacefully protesting African Americans by the white establishment, and to the ways in which the movement ultimately served to promote the common good, views the dynamics of the story primarily in a historical, political, and ethical context, rather than a purely theological one. The rage of the black woman is a rage against injustice, and though her reaction to the paternalistic condescension of an old racist white lady may seem extreme, it is understandable and even justifiable, at least in some measure. Julian's mother's belief in her white supremacy is built on four hundred years of hatred and violence toward blacks (though, of course, she is blind to this), and the African American woman strikes out at that horrific legacy as much as at Julian's mother. O'Connor's counter to this position of sympathy on the reader's part, of course, is Julian, who pretends to believe in racial equality but is, in the end, a worse sinner than his mother on account of his hypocrisy. Julian is a stand-in for the liberal reader who would champion the black woman, at least in principle. The unseemly sight of this terrible son berating his stricken and dying mother at the end of the story is not lost on the reader. You cannot sacrifice your mother on the altar of racial justice—or any other altar, for that matter—without dehumanizing yourself. We are implicated in Julian's psychic and filial violence. So, yes, O'Connor effectively condemns everyone—including Julian's mother who prefers to live in a world based on exploitation of black people rather than one based on equality—but, in many ways, representative racist that she may be, she is not the worst person in the story. Our sympathies are meant to lie with her as she lies dying on the sidewalk while Julian mocks her and the black woman flees back into the darkness she emerged from.

It is precisely at a critical impasse such as this one between intended and perceived meaning in a text that Toni Morrison's vantage point becomes helpful. In *Playing in the Dark*, she describes how she came to appreciate the subtle ways in which the Africanist presence works in American literature: "I began to see how the literature I revered, the literature I loathed, behaved in its encounter with racial ideology. American literature could not help being shaped by that encounter. Yes, I wanted to identify those moments when American literature was complicit in the fabrication of racism, but equally important, I wanted to see when literature exploded and undermined it" (16).

This story, I would suggest, represents one of those occasions when literature works to undermine the author's intended message, suggesting, at one level, what the author means to say, but implying something more besides. Morrison goes on to say that as a writer reading the work of other writers, she came to realize an obvious, and very Freudian, truth: "the subject of the dream is the dreamer. The fabrication of an Africanist persona is reflexive; an extraordinary meditation on the self; a powerful exploration of the fears and desires that reside in the writerly consciousness" (17). Thus seen, the black woman on the bus becomes an embodiment of O'Connor's own fears of black rage and violence, just as she is a fulfillment of Julian's mother's fears of riding the bus alone at night. Published in 1961, well before the more violent events of the civil rights movement, O'Connor's story is strangely prescient, capturing the sense of foreboding much of the white population of the South felt as the old codes that helped people navigate daily life—those "manners" that O'Connor values so highly in her letters, essays, and interviews—dropped away and whites found themselves lost in unexplored territory in terms of the nature of the relationship shared by the races. This lostness is echoed in Julian's mother's final words in the story, as she wanders aimless down the alien sidewalk in a world she no longer belongs to: "'Home,' she muttered.... 'Home,' she said thickly" (*CS* 420). The "home" she longs to return to is not the one she shares with her son, but the world of her childhood, wherein white people, like her grandfather Godhigh, who owned "two hundred slaves," held their rightful place, a world wherein black people were subject and "better off when they were [slaves]" (*CS* 408). O'Connor, of course, does not endorse or romanticize such a world— she is no Margaret Mitchell. But she renders the loss felt by southerners of previous generations, as well as some members of her own, with a poignancy and compassion that the contemporary reader is unlikely to share.

It is also worth noting that O'Connor explores this psychic terrain by means of the parent-child relationship, one that is so central to her own life and one that is central to the lives of all of her characters in the story. In her essay "Aligning the Psychological with the Theological: Doubling and Race in Flannery O'Connor's Fiction," Doreen Fowler points out the many and subtle ways in which the large woman and her son, Carver, serve as black doubles for Julian and his mother, beginning with the fact that both women wear the same hat and following through to Julian identifying the woman as his mother's black double as she lays dying (82). In addition, Julian and Carver (who are both named, interestingly, unlike their mothers who are identified solely by their maternal roles) are reflected images of one another, something Julian himself mentally observes as the large woman sits next to him and Carver sits down next to his mother, noting that "she and the woman had, in a sense, swapped sons" (*CS* 415). As Fowler observes, this doubling functions as a way of blurring the color line that Julian's mother and white people in general have tried so hard to establish and preserve through institutions such as slavery, segregation, and the KKK: "despite white attempts to keep white separate from black, areas of overlap between white and black repeatedly surface in the form of the double" (82). This doubling leads eventually to "violent convergence" of whiteness and blackness, which "topples cultural hierarchy like a house of cards" and returns the characters to the basic human relationship that forms the ground of their selfhood, the parent/child relationship (83). It is both poignant and pathetic that, at the end of the story, Julian, this unappreciative son who has done all he can throughout the story to demean, embarrass, and separate himself from his mother, tries to reclaim her and reestablish the relationship he has secretly wished to sever. As she stumbles away from him in her delirium, not recognizing him as her own, he is reduced to the status of a weeping child: "'Mother! He cried. 'Darling, sweetheart, wait!' Crumpling, she fell to the pavement. He dashed forward and fell at her side, crying, 'Mamma, Mamma!'" (*CS* 420). Meanwhile, the other child in the story, Carver, is wordlessly spirited away by his mother, "the little boy staring wide-eyed over her shoulder," after she has defended him against Julian's mother's paternalistic act, an act she perceives as a form of social violence and an attempt to reestablish the color line that desegregation was designed to erase (*CS* 418). "Teach your children well" is a classic directive that often occurs to me in connection with this story. Though the large black woman is surely mistaken in the lesson she imparts to her child—that one fights violence with violence—she is motivated by the maternal desire to protect her son and clearly means well, as does her white double, Julian's mother, who attempts to pass on her racist vision, rooted in violence, to her son. This is a case of mothers behaving badly, though for different reasons and in different ways—and, in the case of Julian, sons as well.

In addition to the white/black doubling in the story, there is another instance of doubling: the black woman who is Carver's mother and, Caroline, the African American nanny who took care of Julian's mother when she was a child and whom she asks for at the end of the story as she is dying. These two mothers are, in a sense, antitheses of one another. Like the "slave women" that Morrison describes who are rendered "natally dead" to their own children in order to serve as surrogate mothers to white children (21), Caroline embodies a distinctly Africanist mother figure. In response to the conflict with the physical black body of the living, breathing mother-to-her-own-black-child she encounters, Julian's mother flees, in her own mind, to the social black body of her mammy, as well as to the old dispensation, wherein black people occupied a distinct place in the culture and lived their lives in service to whites. Morrison describes this dynamic as that of "the reckless, unabated power of a white woman gathering identity unto herself from the wholly available and serviceable lives of Africanist others" (25). Though when Morrison makes this claim she is analyzing the relationships in Willa Cather's novel *Sapphira and the Slave Girl* rather than in O'Connor's story, the historically grounded predicament holds true. I would also suggest that Morrison's further claim is also applicable: that in exploring these mother-child pairings (Carver and his mother, Julian and his mother, Julian's mother and Caroline) and the power dynamics inherent within each and between them, O'Connor was "dreaming and redreaming her problematic relationship with her own mother" (27), in addition to exploring her own troubled and radically ambivalent relationship to blacks, to the South, and to the civil rights movement.

The parent/child conflict between O'Connor and her mother is well documented by biographers and critics, and it is perhaps most fully recorded by O'Connor herself in her letters, wherein she often regales her correspondents with stories that demonstrate the ways in which she and Regina O'Connor make for poor housemates. While it is true that she thrived on the life she led with her mother at Andalusia, professionally speaking, the conditions of that life were less than ideal. A grown woman with a fiercely independent disposition, she had been forced by her illness to return to live under her mother's roof and was growing more and more dependent on her for her health and well-being each day. This situation would prove challenging to any adult child, but it was particularly difficult given how different the two women were. Regina was a practical person, devoted to farm and family, and also a Southern Lady, with all of the prejudices and provincialism associated with the term. Flannery, on the other hand, was an intellectual (despite her tendencies to make fun of that class of people) and a woman who had escaped the narrowness of her southern upbringing by means of her education at Iowa and her brief time living in New York and Connecticut. Regina would always be an insider in her culture (though her Catholicism set her somewhat apart from her Protestant neighbors). In contrast, Flannery would always be an outsider and an exile. Though, admittedly, as we have seen, she gradually reconverted over the years to a more southern way of seeing and thinking, she was situated *in* the rarified world of rural/small-town Georgia but was not entirely *of* it. Inevitably, mother and daughter did not see eye to eye, causing daily friction between them.

Though one might assume such a scenario would prove a recipe for disastrous family life, this was not the case. As Flannery once quipped, "I come from a family where the only emotion respectable to show is irritation. In some this tendency produces hives, in others literature, in me both" (*HB* 163–64). In fact, O'Connor's stories are full of mothers and daughters (as well as mothers and sons, fathers and sons, fathers and daughters, grandfathers and grandchildren, granduncles and grandnephews) who give each other "hives." The sources of their difference vary greatly, as do the sources of difference from family to family, but the particular dynamic we see in Julian and his mother, between an intelligent or educated daughter/son and a less enlightened mother or that of a daughter/son who is dependent upon a parent ignorant of how to meet the child's needs, shows up again and again in her stories and novels, early and late. In fact, as one considers O'Connor's corpus, it is almost easier to identify stories that do not explore this relationship than those that do, suggesting that for O'Connor the parent/child nexus borders on a kind of creative obsession. As Morrison suggests, the subject of the dream is always the dreamer. What sets "Everything that Rises Must Converge" apart from many of her other stories that feature parents and children (among other things) is that O'Connor images the filial maternal conflict in black and white, employing "surrogate, serviceable" black bodies to participate in the power struggle between mothers and children—as well as between blacks and whites, the troubled southern past and the troubling southern present—from a safe distance.

## The Triumph and Defeat of the Social Black Body: "The Artificial Nigger"

Though the subject of race and the presence of the black body is evident in many of O'Connor's stories, nowhere is it more obvious, from the title onward, than in "The Artificial Nigger," a story O'Connor describes in a letter to Maryat Lee as "My favorite and probably the best thing I'll ever write" (*HB* 209) and a story Morrison acknowledges as a "brilliant... allegory" that engages the serious consequences of black people in white lives (67–68). "The Artificial Nigger" tells the story of a trip to Atlanta made by Mr. Head with his grandson, Nelson, an archetypal journey from the country to the city wherein the travelers acquire essential knowledge about themselves and the world they inhabit. Mr. Head's intention in taking Nelson to Atlanta, the city where he was born but left as an infant, is to teach him a "moral lesson"—that "the city is not a great place," despite the young man's prideful assumptions about his place of origin, and that one of the signs of its moral degeneracy is the presence of "niggers" (*CS* 251). By contrast, the rural town Mr. Head and Nelson live in is void of black people: "There hasn't been a nigger in this county since we run that one out twelve years ago," Mr. Head boasts to ten-year-old Nelson (*CS* 252). As a result of the segregated life he has led, Nelson has never seen a black person, a creature his grandfather harbors a powerful hatred for (as evidenced by his constant use of the dehumanizing word "nigger" to describe African Americans, in contrast to the narrator's consistent use of the word "Negro"), and Mr. Head intends to pass that hatred on. In the course of the story, young Nelson encounters a range of black people, but three black bodies in particular make a powerful impression on him: the "coffee colored" man he sees on the train, the large African American woman he asks directions of when they get lost in the city, and the eponymous statue of an "artificial nigger" Mr. Head and Nelson happen upon at the end of the story. With each of these encounters, we see Nelson move from being an unbiased observer of black physical bodies to acculturation into white ways of perceiving blacks as possessors of social bodies and, therefore, socially constructed blackness. Nelson moves from a state of innocence to one of experience and is successfully, and tragically, indoctrinated by Mr. Head, even as his grandfather begins to receive glimmers of his own culpability for the sin of racism.

Nelson's first encounter with an African American is not what he expects it to be. In the story, the narrator carefully describes the figure of a man making his way down the aisle of the train, channeling Nelson's perspective and observations:

> A huge coffee-colored man was coming slowly forward. He had on a light suit and a yellow satin tie with a ruby pin in it. One of his hands rested on his stomach which rode majestically under his buttoned coat, and in the other he held the head of a black walking stick that he picked up and set down with a deliberate outward motion each time he took a step. He was proceeding very slowly, his large brown eyes gazing over the heads of the passengers. He had a small white mustache and white crinkly hair. Behind him were two young women, both coffee-colored, one in a yellow dress and one in a green. Their progress was kept at a rate of his and they chatted in low throaty voices as they followed him. Mr. Head's grip was tightened insistently on Nelson's arm. As the procession passed them, the light from a sapphire ring on the brown hand that picked up the cane reflected in Mr. Head's eye. (CS 255)

Nelson notices the man's body in full detail and notes most insistently his size (he is "huge," has a "large" stomach and "large" brown eyes) and the details of his clothing, both of which suggest wealth and a level of cultivation well above his own and his grandfather's. The satin tie, the ruby pin, the walking stick, and the sapphire ring, along with the retinue of young women who respectfully follow him in their "procession" down the aisle, invest him with a kind of patriarchal grandeur. The language O'Connor chooses suggests royalty as Nelson, in his innocence, attributes to the man a status that African Americans would never be granted by southern society, and especially by those belonging to the class of poor whites, as he and his grandfather do.

The difference between his unprejudiced perception of the physical black body he beholds and his grandfather's perception of the black man's social body is made immediately apparent a moment later when Mr. Head quizzes Nelson, asking "What kind of man?" he is. In response, Nelson identifies the man's physical traits, describing him as "a fat man" and "an old man." His grandfather triumphantly corrects the boy's supposed blindness, "'That was a nigger,'" an assertion Nelson finds impossible to believe: "You said they were black. . . . You never said they were tan. How do you expect me to know anything when you don't tell me right?" (CS 255). Nelson's question, of course, suggests more than one meaning. Mr. Head is not "telling him right," either in terms of the practical or of the moral instruction he is imparting to his young charge. Nelson does not recognize racial difference until he is taught to by his racist grandfather. O'Connor suggests, through Nelson's objection, that there is no such thing as "blackness," that it is a category invented by white people to distinguish themselves from a despised group of human beings. As Jeanne Perreault notes in her study of "The Artificial Nigger," when Nelson looks at African Americans "he still sees people," unlike his grandfather whose lifelong obsessive categorization has blinded him to blacks as human beings. The old man sees only white people and "niggers." Despite the fact that the coffee-colored man is wealthier than he and dresses better and eats better than he does (as evidenced later in the dining car), Mr. Head considers himself to be superior to him "exclusively because of the color of his skin and his control over the primary signifier ("nigger") that expresses it" (Perreault 396–97). Thus, he later takes delight in showing Nelson the yellow curtain that segregates the coffee-colored man and his family from the main section of the dining car, a car Nelson and he cannot even afford to enter and which they are shooed away from by a bustling black waiter "as if he were brushing aside flies" when they get in his way (CS 256). The curtain exists as a concrete symbol of the color line and the southern code, but in actuality serves as a thin and flimsy assertion of a thin and flimsy cultural myth, that of white superiority.

Nelson's second encounter with black bodies occurs after he and Mr. Head get lost in Atlanta and find themselves in a black neighborhood. Moving from their all-white world, they are intimidated at finding themselves in a different geographical and racial space wherein they constitute a minority and are, thereby, unwelcome objects of curiosity. Both grandfather and grandson note in detail the ubiquity of black people of all shapes and sizes, a sight that both disturbs and fascinates them:

> There were colored men in their undershirts standing in the doors and colored women rocking on the sagging porches. Colored children played in the gutters and stopped what they were doing to look at them. Before long they began to pass rows of stores with colored customers in them but they didn't pause at the entrance of these. Black eyes in black faces were watching them from every direction. (CS 260)

O'Connor's repetition of the word "colored" and her doubling of the word "black" in her rendering of "black eyes in black faces" emphasize both the black bodies of the people they are encountering and the whiteness of Mr. Head and Nelson, whose usually invisible whiteness has suddenly become all too visible, and who, for the first time in their lives, know what it means to be people who do not belong. As Doreen Fowler suggests in an analysis of the story, O'Connor demonstrates in this scene, as well as throughout the story, that racial "Otherness ... is not fixed; rather it is changing, a product of the surrounding environment, and in this environment, white is not superior to black" ("Deconstructing Racial Difference" 24). Indeed, as they seek a way out of the neighborhood, the narrator notes, once again channeling Nelson's perspective, that the "Negroes who were passing" him and his grandfather as they stood on the corner were "going about their business as if they had been white" (CS 262). There is no real difference between the lives of black and white people. Nelson's response to the situation is as much fascination with this similitude and dissimilitude as it is fear of them. Mr. Head, on the other hand, hides his terror of being on unfamiliar ground with white bravado, taking the opportunity to belittle both his grandson and the black people all around him: "Anybody wants to be from this nigger heaven can be from it!" (CS 261). In this context, the term "nigger heaven" takes on significance that Mr. Head may not intend. The presumed meaning is that it is paradise for black people because they are surrounded only by their kind; however, it is also a paradise because there are (ordinarily) no whites present to demean them and enforce unjust, culturally determined restrictions on their freedom. Mr. Head and Nelson perceive that whites are not welcome here, as they smell the "odor of dinners" drifting out to them from the doorways of houses, a tantalizing smell, hungry and lost as they are. They feel the pain and separation of segregation for the first and likely only time in their lives.

Among all these bodies Nelson observes, however, one in particular arrests his attention:

> Up ahead, he saw a large colored woman leaning in a doorway that opened onto the sidewalk. Her hair stood straight out from her head for about four inches all around and she was resting on bare brown feet that turned pink at the sides. She had on a pink dress that showed her exact shape. As they came abreast of her, she lazily lifted one hand to her head and her fingers disappeared into her hair. . . . He stood drinking in every detail of her. His eyes traveled up from her great knees to her forehead and then made a triangular path from the glistening sweat on her neck down and across her tremendous bosom and over her bare arm back to where her fingers lay hidden in her hair. He suddenly wanted her to reach down and pick him up and draw him against her and then he wanted to feel her breath on his face. He wanted to look down and down into her eyes while she held him tighter and tighter. He had never had such a feeling before. He felt as if he were reeling down through a pitchblack tunnel. (CS 261–62)

This description of the large black woman he encounters is central to the story (as is the case with the description of the black mother in "Everything That Rises Must Converge") and is central to our understanding of the way O'Connor construes the female black body. Nelson observes her even more closely than he did the coffee-colored man on the train, noting the fine details of her hair, her hands, her bare brown feet (that, surprisingly, "turn pink at the sides," suggesting that color is not monochrome or monolithic), her knees, her forehead, her neck, her breasts, her bare arm, and, finally, her fingers, which lay hidden in her hair. It is a veritable catalogue of feminine body parts, all of which contribute to making her a mysterious, magnetically attractive presence. The imagery depicts her as damp and voluptuous, a life-giving entity. Nelson, who is hot and thirsty, stands astonished, "drinking in every detail of her" and, breathless with anxiety, longs to "feel her breath on his face." Later, when she speaks to him, he feels "as if a cool spray had been turned on him" (*CS* 262). In addition to the implication that she serves as a kind of oasis in the desert he and his grandfather find themselves in, there is also the suggestion of danger. Nelson's sensation of reeling "down through a pitch-black tunnel" connects with earlier imagery in the story when Mr. Head shows his grandson the sewer system located in the nether regions of the city. When his grandfather pointed this out to him, unintentionally revealing his white male sexual anxiety, Nelson felt both terrified and excited, listening intently to his descriptions of "how a man could slide into it and be sucked along down endless pitchblack tunnels," understanding "for the first time how the world was put together in its lower parts" and triumphantly proclaiming immediately afterward, "This is where I come from!"—a pair of epiphanies that suggest a partial revelation of sexual mystery and the beginning of Nelson's understanding of the sources of his own being (*CS* 259). As Doreen Fowler notes, "The 'pitchblack tunnel' that Nelson conjures is a scarcely veiled image of the vagina/birth canal through which Nelson feels as if he is 'reeling' back to his true place of origin" (26). His identification of the woman with the vagina/birth canal also suggests, however, his inkling that this is connected with his own burgeoning sexuality. Nelson perceives the woman as both a maternal figure—"a mountain of black maternity" in O'Connor's words—and an object of sexual desire (*HB* 78).

Nelson encounters the black woman as he did the coffee-colored man, recognizing the power and presence of her physical body, but, thanks to his grandfather's earlier instruction, the encounter is less innocent. There is something else at work here. In evoking the woman in both maternal and terrifying sexual terms, O'Connor calls up the archetype of the social black female body as both mammy-figure and sexual object. M. Shawn Copeland reminds us of this unsavory history wherein "Slavery thrived on the body of the black woman, which became the site in which the planter's economic desire intersected with black female sex, sexuality, and reproductive capability" (33). Nelson's perception of and response to the black woman is not unlike that of generations of white men who have come before him. He does not see the woman purely, in a detached way; instead, he perceives that the woman is a person who can be of use to him, marking her as an object and her body as one that is socially construed rather than private and individual. *What* she signifies to Nelson is more important than who or what she is independent of his gaze. As a child who lost his mother at the age of one, and as an adult-white-heterosexual-male-in-the-making, Nelson's response to her is far more complicated than his response to the man on the train. Her body engenders desire in him in a way that the body of the man on the train did not and could not. In Morrison's terms, her Africanist presence creates in Nelson a sense of both his Alpha and his Omega, revealing a shadow side of himself he was unaware of before.

The role of the black woman in the story has been much debated among critics and commentators. She is often seen as a stereotype, a figure that serves the purposes of the white characters in the story and, thus, is merely a tool in the fiction writer's hand. For instance, in *The Myth of Aunt Jemima: Representations of Race and Region,* Diane Roberts notes that this figure "typifies the mythic Old South of benign slavery, grace, and abundance" (1). On the other hand, some readers see her, and the implied temptation Nelson feels to cross the color line, as an invitation to miscegenation who, thereby, provides for Nelson an opportunity for recognition of "his common humanity with the Negro woman" (Shackelford 81). Similarly, some critics, such as Claire Kahane, suggest that Nelson's desire serves to blur "the distinction of black and white through sexuality" and thereby obliterates "the entire structure of defined power" upon which Mr. Head's life and the southern ethos he has inherited rests (190). As these varying readings suggest, the figure of the woman is not as straightforward as O'Connor, perhaps, intended her to be. In a letter to a friend, quoted in brief earlier, O'Connor confides that she meant for the woman "in an almost physical way to suggest the mystery of existence to him [Nelson]— he not only has never seen a nigger but he didn't know any women and I felt that such a black mountain of maternity would give him the required shock to start those black forms moving up from his unconscious" (*HB* 78). The "black forms" she speaks of do, indeed, begin to move up "from some dark part of him into the light" (*CS* 264) as the story progresses, so the woman serves as a catalyst to the beginning of his self-knowledge—a point Lucinda H. MacKethan emphasizes in her reading of the story (31). Among the most generous readings along these lines is Robert Brinkmeyer's assertion that the woman is an embodiment of Nelson's hidden self that has at its center "a generosity of spirit towards others" (79). Clearly, insofar as she functions as a symbol, the woman is multifaceted and multivalent. In her analysis of the story, Jeanne Perreault regards the woman as less passive, more active, pointing out that the black woman is given a voice (unlike the man on the train) and accorded a "position of agency" by virtue of her conversation with Nelson (403). When he asks, "How do you get back to town?" she responds playfully, "You in town now" (*CS* 262). The black woman assists Nelson in discovering, physically, where he is. For all of her detachment, her mythic stature and power, she helps to ground Nelson, orient him in the here and now, serving a practical purpose as he makes his mythic journey through Atlanta, the city of his birth. Different as they may be, one point that most of these disparate interpretations agree upon is that the woman's existence is meaningful, finally, only insofar as it serves Nelson's needs. In some ways, they all see her black body as being relative, adjunctive, socially functional and determined.

Nelson and Mr. Head's final encounter with a black body occurs at the conclusion of the story when they come across not an actual body but a representation of one in the form of the "artificial nigger." Having made their way out of the black neighborhood, the two pilgrims find themselves in a less frightening, though equally alien, neighborhood of opulent mansions. Prior to their arrival, Mr. Head has committed what he believes to be an unpardonable sin in denying Nelson in front of a crowd of harpy-like white women who descend upon the child for accidentally running into one of them and knocking her down. Fearing that they might turn him, as the boy's guardian, over to the police or seek restitution for any damages Nelson may have inflicted, he brazenly lies in order to save himself, effectively abandoning his grandchild when he is most vulnerable. The child's need for his grandfather is expressed in powerful bodily terms, as he runs to Mr. Head, who had been hiding from him, "caught him around the hips, and clung panting against him." His grandfather's response to the child's desperate clinging is to "detach Nelson's fingers from the flesh in the back of his legs" and declare, "This is not my boy . . . I never seen him before." Nelson's stunned response is instantaneous as Mr. Head "felt Nelson's fingers fall out of his flesh" (*CS* 265). The listing of specific body parts ("legs," "hips," "fingers") and the repetition of the word "flesh" serve as reminders of the intimate physical nature of the relationship between grandfathers and grandsons—and, by extension, members of the larger human family—of the fact that we are all, in fact, one flesh, and that the denial of one's own is a denial of oneself. Though none of this is ever stated by Mr. Head or Nelson, both understand the significance of the betrayal, and both have a dreadful inkling of the desolate life they are doomed to lead without one another: Mr. Head "felt he knew now what time would be like without seasons and what heat would be like without light and what man would be like without salvation" (*CS* 268). The psychic landscape he wanders through is a barren one, unredeemed by beauty and physical comforts and holding no hope for the future.

It is at this point, at the nadir of their relationship, that Mr. Head and Nelson catch sight of the cryptic figure that distracts them from their shared and separate suffering and enables them to focus on something beyond themselves,

> the plaster figure of a Negro sitting bent over on a low yellow brick fence that curved around a wide lawn. The Negro was about Nelson's size and he was pitched forward at an unsteady angle because the putty that held him to the wall had cracked. One of his eyes was entirely white and he held a piece of brown watermelon.... It was not possible to tell if the artificial Negro were meant to be young or old; he looked too miserable to be either. He was meant to look happy because his mouth was stretched up at the corners but the chipped eye and the angle he was cocked at give him a wild look of misery instead. (*CS* 268)

As with the figure of the black woman, the symbolic significance of the "artificial nigger" has been much discussed, beginning with O'Connor's own confession in one of her letters wherein she states "What I had in mind to suggest with the artificial nigger was the redemptive quality of the Negro's suffering for us all" (*HB* 78). Most critics agree that the statue serves to bring Nelson and Mr. Head together, as the language of the story suggests: "They stood gazing at the artificial Negro as if they were faced with some great mystery, some monument to another's victory that brought them together in their common defeat. They could both feel it dissolving their differences like an action of mercy" (*CS* 269). Ralph Wood asserts that O'Connor achieves her intentions, stating that the sinful grandfather and his equally sinful grandchild, who has held his grandfather's feet to the fire for his betrayal, have "encountered the grace that dissolves all personal and racial hatred" in the figure of the "artificial nigger" (*Comedy of Redemption* 118). However, it is not clear how we are to understand Mr. Head's conversion. Though he evidently feels gratitude for the forgiveness bestowed on him by both Nelson and God, the reader is not certain what he is being forgiven for. Assuredly, he is contrite over his denial of his grandson, but Mr. Head's sins are manifold, and the most besetting of them, arguably, is his hate-filled racism. Though he may be aware of this, at some level, unfortunately, there is no evidence that he has changed his view of black people, as suggested by his insistence on identifying the statue as a "nigger" and by his flippant assessment of why the statue exists in the first place: "They ain't got enough real ones here. They got to have an artificial one" (*CS* 269). "How have [Nelson's and Mr. Head's] attitudes toward blacks been altered?" Frederick Asals asks in his study *Flannery O'Connor: The Imagination of Extremity* (91), a question that inevitably occurs to all readers. The end of the story describes a man cured of his pride and convinced of his depravity; however, it also describes a man who is happy to return to his white world, wherein there are no black people, never to venture forth again. Nelson, who has imbibed his grandfather's lessons throughout the story, from his first sighting of the coffee-colored man on the train (whom he eventually came to hate for his seeming deception in being tan instead of black) to his final encounter with the black statue, seemingly speaks for both of them when he declares at the end of the story, "I'm glad I've went once, but I'll never go back again!" (*CS* 270). No longer the boy who once prided himself on being born in Atlanta, Nelson has learned to despise the city, as his grandfather does, along with the people who inhabit it. Even the train that transports them from their peaceful rural village to the supposedly sin-filled metropolis and back again is imaged as a serpent (*CS* 270), a creature associated with evil and treachery.

Though it has been argued by Wood and others that "neither in art nor in life is the mercy of God a ready panacea for all ills," and that Mr. Head's and Nelson's conversion is partial and, perhaps, the beginning of a new way of conducting themselves in the world, this conclusion to the story leaves the most serious moral problem of the tale unaddressed and therefore seems to belie O'Connor's intentions, both the ones she openly expresses and the ones that are implied in the story (*Comedy of Redemption* 118). Nelson's third and final encounter with a black body is radically unlike the first two in that the "artificial nigger" is a representation of a black social body rather than an interaction with a physical body, an actual human being. The statue, as an invention of a (presumably) white artisan is the product of a white imagination—a white idea of a black person—and has no basis in reality. Rather than being composed of flesh and blood, it is made of inert materials and is, therefore, not human—a fact that suggests, metaphorically, the dehumanization black people have been subject to by whites for centuries. The statue has no name, no individual identity, and exists only as a social construction of blackness and otherness. The few physical features he is given suggest the condition of the black man in the South; he is ageless (black men are treated as children, referred to as "boy"), emasculated, stereotyped as a thief (as the watermelon might suggest), and, most significant of all, forced to wear a mask of contentment in the presence of white people, despite his inner misery. This Africanist presence, which supposedly induces contrition and conversion in the errant pilgrims, according to O'Connor, mostly seems to produce puzzlement and the certain conviction that they never want to deal with a live black body again.

In addition, the equivalency that O'Connor seems to suggest in positing that the "negro's" suffering belongs to and is redemptive for all human beings constitutes a kind of appropriation many contemporary readers object to. This is akin to the problem raised by O'Connor's wishing "a plague on everybody's house as far as the race business goes" in her story "Everything That Rises Must Converge," claiming blacks and whites are equally culpable for the actions that unfold since all are equally subject to Original Sin. Speaking in terms of O'Connor's theology, Original Sin is indeed responsible for the black woman's rage on the bus, but it is also responsible for slavery, the centuries-long systematic dehumanization of black people by whites. These are by no means equivalent sins, and lumping them together under the same theological category of human behavior compromises our ability to see our history, the actions that constitute it, and our own collective and private moral culpability clearly. In her study of the role of place (both geographic and social) in O'Connor's texts, Laurel Nesbitt describes O'Connor's tendency to invoke theological explanations for the social issues she dramatizes in her stories as evidence of the ways in which her whiteness blinds her: "By elaborating so eloquently on the social issues of her time, and by simultaneously and stubbornly insisting that her texts are about theology before they are about the social, O'Connor exposes her own position both as a Catholic and as a white woman of relative privilege who has no real investment in change in the post–World War II South" (9).

These same dynamics might be seen in the conclusion of "The Artificial Nigger." First, there is the theological solution to the social problem. As Timothy P. Caron notes in his study of what he terms O'Connor's "theological whiteness," "When O'Connor tells us that she meant for a piece of racist lawn statuary to suggest 'the redemptive quality of the Negro's suffering for us all,' then we are free to displace the messy topic of race from our readings and firmly fix our gaze upon heaven, for it is there that race will cease to matter" (162). In addition, we see O'Connor's signature gesture toward creating unity between blacks and whites through their common suffering. While it is true that all human beings suffer, regardless of race, the extraordinary and particularly horrific suffering that has been visited upon black people in America has been borne by them in addition to the ordinary suffering that comes with being human. In her essay "The Artificial Niggers," Claire Kahane demonstrates the problem of not recognizing this historical and social reality. The fact that O'Connor "appropriates the ready-made stereotype" of the "sentimentalized... portrayal of 'the Negro' as a passive, long-suffering figure" and uses it "as a metaphor of redemptive humility" essentially tries to equate the unequal suffering of whites and blacks, to create the illusion of an equality that whites do not believe in, and to make the false claim that "We are all niggers" (184). O'Connor's attempt to meld white and black suffering, might be seen, in Morrison's terms, as an attempt on the part of a white author to claim a "serviceable, surrogate" black body (in this case, a representation of that body in the form of the statue) "in behalf of her own desire for a *safe* participation in loss, in love, in chaos, in justice" (28; emphasis Morrison's)—or at least on behalf of her desire for her white characters' participation. While it may be true that black bodies and white bodies have all experienced defeat, the nature of the defeat they have suffered is not something they hold in "common." Those experiences are radically unlike, separate and unequal, as different and divergent as black and white.

## Disruptive Black Bodies: "The Geranium" and "Judgement Day," Reprise

As the analyses of "The Geranium" and "Judgement Day" in the Introduction and Chapter 1 suggest, the presence of an Africanist Other in the life of Old Dudley and T. C. Tanner disrupts both white men's sense of the relationship between the races. Each experiences an encounter with a black man's body in the stairwell of the New York apartment building where he lives, and each man dies as a result (both direct and indirect) of that encounter. This experience runs counter to the relationship each man enjoyed with his Africanist Other when he lived in the South, respectively Rabie and Coleman—relationships that were life-giving (at least for the white man) and that respected the color line. Part of the difference between the dispensations the white men enjoyed in the South and rued in the North lies in the fact that Rabie's and Coleman's black bodies were socially constructed while the black bodies of the African American men in the stairwell were encountered in a physical way. As different as the two northern blacks are in the two versions of the story—the first being condescending and conciliatory, the second being angry and hostile—they are alike in that they establish an unwelcome intimacy with their white counterparts through the agency of touch. The kindly meant pat on the back from a black man proves to be as devastating as a violent attack suffered at a black man's hands. Both Dudley and Tanner are destroyed by the violation of the norms they know and their encounter with black bodies.

There is an additional layer of complexity and cause for disruption in "Judgement Day" as O'Connor introduces additional Africanist Others into the story, most notably the black actor's girlfriend, who is tangentially involved in the violence that breaks out between the two men. Tanner (like Nelson in "The Artificial Nigger") is both drawn to and appalled by this highly sexualized black female body, described by the narrator as "a young tan-skinned woman with bright copper-colored hair" (CS 542). He watches as she and the actor flirt in the hallway, "The Negro was grinning. He took a swipe at one of her hips" (CS 543). Tanner is almost jubilant as he delivers the report to his daughter a few minutes later that the new neighbor "got him this high-yeller, high-stepping woman with red hair" (CS 543). While it may be true that Tanner has long prided himself on "knowing how to handle niggers," he knows nothing about women, white or black, as his dysfunctional relationship with his daughter would suggest. Thus, unlike her partner, whom Tanner assumes he understands, identifying him (incorrectly, of course) as a preacher from Alabama, she remains a source of mystery to him as well as a source of anxiety. The day after he first encounters the couple, Tanner experiences a brief moment alone with the woman:

> He was standing in the hall early the next morning when the woman came out of her door alone, walking on high gold-painted heels. He wished to bid her good morning or simply to nod but instinct told him to beware. She didn't look like any kind of woman, black or white, he had ever seen before and he remained pressed against the wall, frightened more than anything else, and feigning invisibility. (CS 544)

Tanner's wariness is precipitated by the woman's sexual power. Rather than seeming garish, the glittering gold heels she walks in seem to give her a kind of stature, to set her on a pedestal of some sort, as she flaunts her body unabashedly. The use here of archaic language, his wish to "bid her good morning," suggests a courtliness on Tanner's part that is not typical of this crude man who enjoyed, when he lived in the South, threatening his black workers at knifepoint. Up until now, she has been entirely determined for him by her sexual availability (she cohabits with a man she is probably not married to), her light skin (a trait associated with loose women, since under the rule of slavery light-skinned women often became the concubines of white men), and her dyed red hair (a color traditionally associated with promiscuity and rarely associated with black people). Also, because of her white features, her black body crosses the color line, challenging the old man's assumptions about what constitutes blackness and what black and white behavior should look like. His sense of the color line he once lived by is blurred by her physical appearance, and he is unable to categorize her using the usual codes that would make of her body a purely social construction. As a result, Tanner is intimidated by her and tries to hide his white male presence. A man who has spent much of his life trying to invest himself with visibility and power before black people is suddenly—and voluntarily—rendered invisible by a black woman.

In his final violent encounter on the stairwell with his black nemesis, Tanner encounters the woman for the third and final time. Likely suffering from the onset of the stroke that will kill him, Tanner has fallen down the steps. When he reaches out for help from the black actor, who happens to be walking by, the nameless tan woman is at his side, her face "pale, topped with a pile of copper-glinting hair and twisted as if she had just stepped in a pile of dung" (CS 549). This final, shocking image of the woman seems gratuitously hideous. Previously in the story, Tanner's disapproval of her is evident, but so is his attraction—an attraction that has seemingly morphed into utter aversion. This implied association of sexuality with human excretion is also evident, though in less repugnant form, in "The Artificial Nigger" in Nelson's sense of the connection between the large black woman he is powerfully attracted to in a black neighborhood in Atlanta and the sewers that run beneath the streets. The "endless pitchblack tunnels" that lead to his understanding "for the first time how the world was put together in its lower parts" (CS 259) and his sensation of being pulled into one of those tunnels when he meets her constitutes a kind of sexual awakening for Nelson, but it is also inevitably tinged with distasteful bodily functions—a reality that O'Connor chronicles consistently throughout the story, from the chamber pot glinting in the moonlight in the opening scene to the Heads' outhouse, the fancy indoor toilets Mr. Head shows Nelson in Atlanta, and the lurid description of the sewers (Perreault 398). O'Connor, incarnational writer that she is, highlights in grotesque ways the fact that we are embodied creatures, flawed, broken, and ugly (at times), reminding us that our ugliness cannot be separated from our beauty. The last distorted and distorting glimpse Tanner has of the attractive black body he has watched with rapt attention reminds him not of birth and maternal fecundity, as it might a young boy at the beginning of his life, but, instead, fulfills the function of a *memento mori*, offering the old man an image of death and decay, returning him to the ground of his being and unbeing even as he breathes his last breath.

## The Destabilizing Presence of the Africanist Other

As is evident in these reinterpretations of "Everything That Rises Must Converge," "The Artificial Nigger," "The Geranium," and "Judgement Day," viewing her stories through the lens Morrison provides readers with in *Playing in the Dark* demonstrates O'Connor's preoccupation with the destabilizing effect of black bodies on white lives. The black bodies encountered by Julian and his mother, Nelson and Mr. Head, Old Dudley, and T. C. Tanner present a radical challenge to their perceptions of the world and irreparably alter their lives. Much as they may wish to, they cannot return to the state of willful ignorance they once enjoyed. Though still partially blinded by their whiteness, they perceive at least a glimpse of a new dispensation—or, more precisely, a dispensation that had always existed but they were unaware of—one in which race is a relative rather than an absolute condition, and one wherein they are bound in mysterious ways to the black bodies they previously despised or simply failed to see. They may try to reject this terrible new knowledge, but what is seen cannot be unseen.

Viewing these stories through this lens creates a similarly destabilizing effect on readers and critics of O'Connor's work. Stories we may be accustomed to seeing in a particular way become less clear, more complicated, as new meanings and new ways of meaning become available. Considering the complexity of the role played by black bodies in O'Connor's fiction challenges some of the more conventional, received readings, even as it raises questions about O'Connor's level of consciousness and control over these dynamics. This may lead to uneasiness on the part of some readers. There is a natural desire to defend the writers one admires against suggestions that they may not unerringly make the best choices, be they moral or artistic. However, O'Connor does not need our defense. Such is the power and authority of her work that it withstands scrutiny and, in fact, becomes richer and fuller the more we subject it to hard questions.

In *Playing in the Dark*, Morrison issues a challenge to readers of O'Connor, and of other great American writers, as well: "All of us, readers and writers, are bereft when criticism remains too polite or too fearful to notice a disrupting darkness before its eyes" (91). The issue of race constitutes both a disrupting darkness and an abiding presence in O'Connor's work. Though it may be true that she deals with the subject of race with varying degrees of penetration and discernment from story to story and that she achieves varying levels of success in portraying the complexity of racial dynamics, the bottom line is that she looked hard at what is hard to look at and refused to look away. O'Connor struggled to write about this supremely difficult subject during one of the most challenging periods in American history and in the history of the South, in particular. Exploration of O'Connor's representation of race in these stories, and others, provides a sense of the power and probing honesty of her work. As an artist, Flannery O'Connor was neither "fearful" nor "polite." We honor her work by reading it in the spirit in which it was written.

# 5 / The Failure and Promise of Communion

It would be inaccurate to suggest that Flannery O'Connor's handling of race in her stories is universally disruptive and constrained by the blindness of whiteness. It is my hope that the preceding chapters recognize her accomplishment in addressing this difficult subject in her fiction with courage and honesty, despite her radical ambivalence and the limitations she herself is aware of. This is true of many of her predecessors, as well—great writers whose whiteness prevented them from understanding and engaging blackness with the same authoritative vision with which they could see and present the white world. O'Connor's challenge is the same one faced by white American writers of every era, each of whom meets it in his or her unique way, creating fiction that engages the social realities of the time and responds to the dictates of the individual imagination. Given the history of African Americans in the United States, no writer who seeks to capture the reality of American culture can afford not to address the question of race. According to Ralph Ellison, American writers "who stereotype or ignore the Negro or other minorities in the final analysis stereotype and ignore their own humanity" (*Shadow and Act* 60). White Americans must attempt to understand black Americans in order to understand themselves. To know "the Negro" (in Ellison's terms) is to know oneself, difficult and partial as that knowing may be. This principle is implicit in O'Connor's fiction, and it manifests primarily in the ways in which white and black people succeed and fail at communication and communion.

One of those white literary predecessors who addressed his attention to matters of race is Herman Melville, who famously coined the phrase the "power of blackness" to describe the dark knowledge of Original Sin that lent Nathaniel Hawthorne's stories such penetrating insight ("Hawthorne and His Mosses" 243). O'Connor also admired Hawthorne's fiction, acknowledged him as "a very great writer" (*HB* 70), and channeled his work and disposition, as did Melville, in a number of ways. Indeed, in a letter to William Sessions, she refers to their shared tendency to write stories that portray the coalescence of the natural and the supernatural in everyday human life and demonstrate a preoccupation with mystery, acknowledging, "Hawthorne said he didn't write novels, he wrote romances; I am one of his descendants" (*HB* 407). All three writers share a fascination with the darker aspects of the human soul and the compelling need to probe it. For Melville in particular, "blackness" became a symbol for the presence of mystery, while whiteness (as expressed in the celebrated chapter of *Moby Dick* titled "The Whiteness of the Whale") is a symbol, in the apt summation of Toni Morrison, of all that is "mute, meaningless, unfathomable, pointless, frozen, veiled, curtained, dreaded, senseless, implacable" (*Playing in the Dark* 59). The fact that the idea of blackness was instantiated in a race of human beings provided Melville with a metaphorical means of exploring our common mystery, possessed by both black and white people, as one might come to know oneself through knowledge of The Other. This is not unlike the pattern we have seen in O'Connor's stories wherein white characters arrive at a fuller self-knowledge through an encounter with a black double. This encounter is nearly always one of tension and opposition rather than communion, though it will become evident later in the chapter that communion sometimes, if rarely, actually takes place.

In his brilliant novella *Benito Cereno*, Melville portrays a version of black/white communion as it conveys the tale of the eponymous Spanish captain whose ship has been taken over by the slaves it carries. The ship is boarded by an American, Captain Delano, who is blissfully unaware that the insurrection has taken place—for the slaves are engaged in an elaborate pantomime, pretending to be the subject creatures the white man expects them to be, whereas in reality, the Spanish crew is being held in check by the threat of violence. This pantomime constitutes an ingenious flipping of the performative roles the racial code demands of blacks and whites, even as the Africans on board pretend to their subservient status. In a powerful metaphor for the situation, the leader of the insurrection, Babo, is depicted as shaving Benito Cereno, holding a blade against his master's throat, only instead of performing an act of servitude, he wields the power of life and death, effectively reversing the master-slave relationship and making Babo a black version of Benito. Later in the novella, when the dense Delano—whose typically American naiveté is outstripped only by his white blindness, never really seeing black people for who and what they truly are—discovers and quells the insurrection, he asks the sick and dying Benito Cereno what has so darkened his vision and drained him of the desire to live: "'You are saved,' cried Captain Delano, more and more astonished and pained; 'you are saved: what has cast such a shadow upon you?'" Cereno's response consists of only two words: "The negro" (116). In terms of the story, Cereno is undone by the realization of the humanity of the creatures he has been trafficking in and of his own inhumanity in laboring under the delusion that they aren't human at all. His is a rude awakening to the fact of having been blinded by his whiteness. His words, then, also serve as a warning to Delano—and to all Americans—of the beam that is still in the collective eye of a country that has enslaved black people for hundreds of years and believed, somehow, that their souls would not be sickened by this practice. Melville wrote his novella in 1855, six years ahead of the bloody war that would be fought in defense of this brutal institution. Eight years before the Emancipation Proclamation, the nation Melville's story challenges still officially regards African Americans as chattel and nonpersons. Cereno's last words are thus prophetic as well as descriptive of America's current condition. "Negro," of course, is Spanish for "black." He dies as he cryptically warns the wondering Delano of the darkness that will soon engulf the collective soul of his country, a darkness specifically associated with the black man and America's treatment of him.

It is worth noting that Ralph Ellison, a contemporary of O'Connor, chose to invoke Melville's novella and his uncanny encapsulation of America's racial dilemma in his signature novel *Invisible Man*, echoing Captain Delano's question in an epigraph. In fact, the book effectively begins with the benighted white man's words, posing a question that is answered not by Cereno's cryptic and multivalent response (which the author omits) but by Ellison's own tale of a black man who is never properly seen, let alone understood, by whites. In the world of Ellison's novel, the shadow of "the Negro" that haunts Captain Delano haunts everyone—the African American narrator and protagonist of the story, whose blackness both defines him and estranges him from himself, as well as the characters he encounters, both white people and black, on account of the fearful history between the races in America. That history is defined by violence, beginning with the original violence inflicted by whites on slaves and continuing to the present moment, wherein the narrator sits, holed up in his Harlem apartment, listening to Louis Armstrong singing "What Did I Do to Be So Black and Blue?" and living the legacy of that original violence (7). America's violent racial past is very much evident in its violent racial present, in Ellison's world and in our own, though few white people acknowledge this continuum, choosing, instead, to remain (like Captain Delano) ignorant of our shared darkness.

O'Connor, however, like Melville and Ellison, at once perceived this darkness and harnessed its power to fuel her fiction. Unlike many of her southern counterparts and some of her fellow southern writers—including, most famously, fellow Georgian Margaret Mitchell, whose blockbuster *Gone with the Wind* occasionally serves as the butt of O'Connor's jokes—she had no nostalgia for the racial dispensation of the past or for the faux heroism of the Civil War and did not imaginatively participate in its mighty mythos. In one of her letters, she writes ironically, "We have been undergoing big doings here on account of Secession was passed in M'ville 100 years ago. A pageant for 3 days and a big parade in 20 degree weather with young ladies on floats freezing in their drafty dresses, etc. etc. Long live the Wah Between the States" (*HB* 428). O'Connor was as unromantic in her attitude about the war as it is possible to be, despite the participation of her famed and locally celebrated ancestors and the fact that she was named for one of them, Confederate officer Captain John Flannery (Gooch 15). As with contemporary politics, O'Connor does not often choose the South's troubled history as the focus for her fiction, but on the occasions when she does address it, she subverts nostalgia.

In the story that most directly engages the subject of the Civil War, "A Late Encounter with the Enemy," O'Connor mercilessly skewers the generation of old soldiers who are hailed as "Glorious upright old [men] standing for the old traditions! Dignity! Honor! Courage!" but who are, in reality, imposters (*CS* 135). The protagonist, 104-year-old General Sash, is so old he has forgotten his own true past and has substituted the fictional cultural narrative that has supplanted it. Though he was likely a foot soldier—if, indeed, he ever participated in the war at all—Sash imagines himself to be an officer ever since he was given a general's uniform twelve years before to wear at the premiere of a Civil War film (clearly *Gone with the Wind*, though O'Connor leaves the movie unnamed): "I was in that preemie they had in Atlanta," he habitually brags, "It was nothing local about it" (*CS* 136). Sash is ultimately relieved of his amnesia, however, at the climax of the story as he suffers a stroke while seated onstage at his granddaughter's graduation. As the darkness of death descends upon him, he is beset by glimpses of his inglorious past, and "a succession of places—Chickamauga, Shiloh, Marthasville—rushed at him as if the past were the only future now and he had to endure it" (*CS* 142).

Forced to face the violence he inflicted and suffered—and has suppressed for nearly a century—the "general" gives up the false version of the war he has been deluded by for so long and collapses beneath the weight of the real one. The final glimpse of Sash O'Connor gives the reader is of the uniformed old man slumped in his wheelchair, accompanied by John Wesley, the fat Boy Scout assigned to the duty of escorting him: "The crafty scout had bumped him out the back way and rolled him at high speed down a flagstone path and was waiting now, with the corpse, in the long line at the Coca-Cola machine" (CS 144). O'Connor's satire at the expense of her native Southland, and of her state in particular, is palpable in this absurd pairing of final images as one southern institution—the mythos of the Civil War, as aggrandized by Margaret Mitchell's novel and the subsequent film, both set largely in Atlanta—gives way to another—Coca-Cola, a product invented and produced in Georgia. Though the two symbols of the South may seem to be associated with different eras—the Old South, whose passing is represented by the dead general, and the New South, whose identity as a thriving capitalist/manufacturing hub is represented by the Coke machine—it's a noteworthy fact of history that the inventor of Coca-Cola was Confederate Lieutenant Colonel John Stith Pemberton, a pharmacist from Columbus, Georgia, who concocted the first incarnation of the drink in his quest to find a substitute for the morphine he habitually took to relieve the pain of the wounds he had suffered in the war (Blanding 13–14). The present is inevitably shadowed by the past, and in the South, everything is shadowed by the war, even the seemingly innocent and progressive image of Coca-Cola.

O'Connor understood not only the darkness cast by the war itself but also the darkness cast by what made it necessary in the first place—the sin of slavery. In a speech O'Connor gave upon receiving the Georgia Writers' Association Award for *The Violent Bear It Away*, O'Connor alludes to this darkness as a source of power for her own fiction and for southern writers in general:

> When Walker Percy won the National Book Award, newsmen asked him why there were so many good Southern writers and he said, "Because we lost the War." He didn't mean by that simply that a lost war makes good subject matter. What he was saying is that we have had our Fall. We have gone into the world with an inburnt knowledge of human limitations and with a sense of mystery which could not have developed in our first state of innocence—as it has not sufficiently developed in the rest of our country. (*MM* 59)

O'Connor's claiming of the Civil War is akin to Benito Cereno's claiming of "The negro"—once the dark knowledge of one's complicity in evil becomes evident, one cannot return to a state of innocence. The South is defined by its past, just as surely as humankind, according to the Judeo-Christian mythos O'Connor subscribes to, is defined by Original Sin, the fall from grace, and the constant need for redemption. O'Connor and Percy, both of whom are devoted Catholics, see the war in theological terms and lay claim to the collective guilt they and their fellow southerners have incurred. In fact, O'Connor refers to the South as "the land of sin and guilt" in one of her letters to Maryat Lee (albeit half-jokingly), a phrase related to another of her formulations along these lines that she uses with some frequency, referring to the region of her birth as "the dear old dirty Southland" (*HB* 475, 266, 461, 537).

However, it should be noted that even this claim bespeaks a white perspective. As John D. Sykes Jr. notes in his study of O'Connor's relationship to the Agrarians, "The 'we' Percy had in mind was white, and in approvingly quoting his answer in 'The Regional Writer,' O'Connor registers her own unrecognized racial orientation" (38). The outcome of the Civil War was surely a loss for white people in the South, but it constituted a victory for black people. For the freed slaves, the war was not a tragedy but a cause for celebration, not a sign of bondage to one's irrevocable past but the freedom from bondage and the promise of a better future. (At least this is what the abolition of slavery meant theoretically. As history unfolded, however, it would take many decades for the fullness of that promised freedom to come to into being.) Indeed, to put this in terms of Melville's story, had the slave who led the insurrection aboard Benito Cereno's ship survived and been asked the question Delano poses to Cereno, surely Babo would have responded, "The White Man." Perspective determines how one sees the world, a basic truth that is essential to keep in mind when reading O'Connor's—or any—fiction.

As we have seen, O'Connor's art is informed by her unique and particular view of history, theology, politics, race, and local culture. In order to enter into the world of any artist, it is necessary to grant the artist her vision, even and perhaps especially when it does not conform to our own. Some of the many questions that a study like this one raises might be posed as follows: Where do we find truth in this vision? How does it challenge our own contemporary beliefs? Can a work still speak to us, even if and when it is inflected by racial biases that have been exposed and that we are consciously trying to eradicate? Clearly, these are questions that can be asked—and have been asked—of every writer in every age, from Homer to Shakespeare (whose *Othello* and *Merchant of Venice* continue to speak to us in fraught and complex ways) to Melville and O'Connor, and down to the writers of our own present moment. As the analyses of her stories in previous chapters have suggested, O'Connor has much to offer the reader in terms of an understanding of race relations in America, especially as seen from a white perspective. This is enlightening for all readers, white and black, and constitutes one of the reasons O'Connor's fiction continues to appeal to us.

## The Failure of Communion: "The Enduring Chill"

As was suggested earlier in this chapter, one of the most persistent themes that emerges from O'Connor's stories with regard to race relations is the repeated failure of communion between black people and white. Time and time again, moments of potential communication open up in the stories but are then closed down, usually through a willful action on the part of the human beings involved. This pattern became evident in the earlier discussion of "Revelation," wherein Mrs. Turpin reveals the terrible message she received in the doctor's office to the field hands she is offering water to, a secret that is greeted with the black pantomime of outrage rather than genuine compassion. One might see the interactions of Old Dudley and T. C. Tanner in "The Geranium" and "Judgement Day" with the black men in the hallway as instances of miscommunication, moments of potential communion lost to them, largely due to their own prejudices and insufficiencies. In "Everything That Rises Must Converge," Julian attempts to ingratiate himself with a black man on the bus reading a newspaper, but the man rebuffs his attempts, choosing to remain safely ensconced behind the paper wall he has erected. It is as if he knows the white man's self-serving reasons for seeking him out (as do we, being privy to Julian's thoughts), that the communion he thinks he desires is not genuine. Julian simply wants to use the man to demonstrate his supposed racial tolerance and to irritate his racist mother. In "The Barber," Rayber wants to hear what "the boy" George's politics are and is frustrated by the black man's predictable response as George claims he would vote for the conservative (and racist) candidate, a statement made solely to appease his white employer. In each of these stories, black people are guarded, aware that their power (insofar as they possess any) lies in protecting their inviolable privacy. We are reminded of O'Connor's characterization of the "Southern Negro" as "a man of very elaborate manners and great formality which he uses superbly for his own protection" (*MM* 234). The unspoken conviction behind the actions of black people is that white people are not to be trusted.

This pattern plays itself out perhaps most visibly in "The Enduring Chill," the story of a young man, Asbury Fox, who returns to his mother's farm after living in New York, afflicted with a mysterious disease and convinced that he is dying. While up North, Asbury has absorbed liberal views on race and brings them with him when he returns home, only to find that they have no place in the segregated South. On a previous visit home, Asbury had been working on a play about "the Negro," and in an effort "to see how they really felt about their condition," he tries to ingratiate himself with the two black dairymen, Morgan and Randall, who work for his mother (*CS* 368). Clearly suspicious of the white man, they regard him warily. O'Connor captures deftly the quiet refusal of the black men to engage in any genuine communication with Asbury, depicting the subtle dynamics of their conversation: "When they said anything to him, it was as if they were speaking to an invisible body located to the right or left of where he actually was" (*CS* 368). The image here is instructive in that the two black men conduct themselves according to the southern racial code, addressing a mental construct of their white employer's son rather than the man himself. They are playing at communication—and playing Asbury, the would-be playwright—rather than actually engaging in it. This also allows them to avoid eye contact with him. Both men are acculturated in the ways of the South. As Matthew Day points out in his study of the southern code of manners in O'Connor's work, "With an economy of expression that the genre of the short story demands, O'Connor reveals a world where black men receive death sentences simply for looking white men in the eyes" (137). In addition to danger, eye contact invites intimacy, and intimacy with this young man who is trying to use them to achieve his own ends is the last thing Morgan and Randall wish to cultivate.

Asbury finally bribes them into acknowledging him when he offers each of them a cigarette, and as the three of them stand smoking in the dairy (an activity strictly forbidden by Asbury's exacting mother, whose authority he challenges at every turn) he internally celebrates his success: "It was one of those moments of communion when the difference between black and white is absorbed into nothing" (*CS* 368). As with Julian on the bus, the humor of the moment is palpable as this supposed liberal imagines a scenario that could not be further from reality. Morgan and Randall, who have to put up with Asbury and his ineptitude in the dairy on account of the fact that he is the boss's son, do not forget for a moment the difference between black and white—and neither does Asbury, who considers himself a rather fine fellow as he condescends to work with and now smoke with African Americans. By inserting himself into the work lives of the two black men and trespassing into their space, Asbury is, in fact, enacting his white privilege, as surely as is the white person who chooses to move into a black neighborhood in order to demonstrate his or her racial tolerance or color blindness (Sullivan 10). He is no more welcome or wanted than Mr. Head or Nelson are in the African American neighborhood in downtown Atlanta or than Julian is by the black businessman on the bus. It is only by virtue of their whiteness that they have the freedom to trespass—a freedom black people do not have. Asbury, of course, is blind to the racial dynamics of the scenario and in his ignorance savors this faux communion. One can practically imagine the scene that he will write when he sits down to work the moment into his play.

O'Connor, of course, is having a good deal of fun with the character, as he is, once again, a version of herself. Having returned to the South suffering from a mysterious disease (only in her case, the affliction is real), having been exposed to northern values that do not translate into southern culture, and living as a writer who takes her material from the people around her, O'Connor knows Asbury's predicament intimately. The difference between them is that she knows that the relationship between blacks and whites is intractable. Any kind of "communion" established is going to be an illusion, a pathetic pantomime on both sides. Asbury's crossing of the color line doesn't end with violence—as it almost assuredly would have had the black men in question done the crossing—but it does make him sick. In trying to repeat their brief moment of communion, Asbury invites the two dairymen to drink raw milk with him from the same cup he drinks from. Both men refuse, ostensibly because Asbury's mother forbids it. He persists in urging them to drink, believing that their reluctance is race-based: "Listen . . . the world is changing. There's no reason I shouldn't drink after you or you after me!" (*CS* 369), Asbury says, heroically (to his mind) rejecting the Jim Crow rules Morgan and Randall are bound by. The true situation, however, emerges later. As dairymen they know that the milk is tainted, and, in fact, it is Asbury's partaking of it that eventually causes his mysterious illness (ultimately diagnosed as undulant fever, the result of drinking unpasteurized milk) and precipitates his return from New York. But Asbury doesn't quit. Before the diagnosis is announced, in one more desperate bid for their attention, he asks to have them present at his bedside as he endures what he believes are his final hours of suffering. The two men arrive, clearly embarrassed, forced into a condition of intimacy with this white man they neither know nor trust. They stand awkwardly, grinning, shuffling, and assuring him that he looks well—donning their conciliatory masks—a source of irritation to a man who thinks he is dying. In attempt to replicate their moment of communion, he holds out a package of cigarettes. However, he forgets to shake them out, and the comic result of his solemn gesture ensues: "The Negro took the package and put it in his pocket. 'I thank you,' he said. 'I certainly do prechate it'" (CS 379). Randall has no desire to smoke with Asbury, but he will happily accept the seeming gift he offers and smoke alone. Asbury realizes this when he sees Morgan's face turn sullen, and then responds by giving him, too, a package of cigarettes. The men stand around, miserable for the next few minutes, enduring their purgatorial visit, doing everything they can to avoid meaningful communication: "Neither of them seemed to find a suitable place to rest his gaze" (CS 380). Finally, Asbury calls to his mother, who had left him alone, at his request, but is now annoyed at her neglect: "It was apparent she had no intention of getting rid of them for him" (CS 380).

Asbury's attempts at communion fail, in part, because he is not sincere in his interest in them, and the black men know this. The dynamic O'Connor portrays here is part of an age-old pattern of racial miscommunication in America. James Baldwin, with whom O'Connor disagreed so fervently on matters having to do with civil rights, captures this same dynamic powerfully and poignantly in *The Fire Next Time*:

> The Negro came to the white man for a roof or for five dollars or for a letter to the judge: the white man came to the Negro for love. But he was not often able to give what he came seeking. The price was too high; he had too much to lose. And the Negro knew this, too. When one knows this about a man, it is impossible for one to hate him, but unless he becomes a man—becomes equal—it is also impossible for one to love him. (102)

It is surprising, perhaps, as well as strangely true that the object O'Connor's white characters desire when they seek out communion with blacks, from Old Dudley through to T. C. Tanner, is love. They want to be admired, to be valued, to be affirmed in their superior role, and perhaps even to be understood by black people. In their white blindness, they do not understand why this is not possible. Their self-love prevents them from seeing how utterly unlovable they are. Black people, by contrast, see this very clearly—both as they are characterized in O'Connor's stories and in Baldwin's essay. Here we witness O'Connor and Baldwin—white person and black person, conservative and liberal, woman and man, southerner and northerner—looking at black-white relations from their different perspectives and seeing the same thing. Both also perceive that the black man is too wise—and too conditioned by experience—to seek out or expect love from whites. As Baldwin asserts, until there is genuine equality, an equality that is understood and consciously embraced by whites, communion cannot happen. That human beings had not arrived at such a place in 1958, when O'Connor's story was written, or in 1963, when Baldwin's essay was written, is a source of concern to both writers, as evidenced by their preoccupation with this theme. That we still have not arrived at this place now, a half-century later, after being governed for eight years by America's first black president, after living in an era wherein violence toward blacks by America's police departments spawned the Black Lives Matter movement, and after witnessing the resurgence of white supremacist organizations around the country is more than a source of concern. American culture in the early twenty-first century is still poised at the same impasse that O'Connor and Baldwin portray and describe. The "manners" may have changed, to use O'Connor's word—the particular ways of conducting our miscommunication—but the failure to communicate and the failure of communion still haunts relationships between whites and blacks in America. Slavery, the Civil War, Jim Crow, white supremacy, the civil rights movement, and Black Lives Matter—all of which might be summed up in Benito Cereno's words, "The negro"—continue to figure largely in our cultural memory and our society. As long as they do, O'Connor's stories will be relevant and telling.

## A Vision of Communion: *The Violent Bear It Away*

Though O'Connor's vision of the relationship between the races is conveyed in local, particular terms, it is part of a grander vision of humanity. As I discussed briefly in Chapter 3, one of O'Connor's major influences was the work of Teilhard de Chardin. Teilhard's vision of the gradual divinization of humanity and the world is one of powerful hope, expressed even in the face of the fact of entropy (Teilhard was a scientist who understood the ways in which the earth was breaking down) and in the face of man made catastrophe (including World War I, World War II, and the Holocaust). The cosmic convergence of all things and all people, subsumed in the image of the crucified Christ, the divine force made incarnate in the world in order to redeem it, was an end O'Connor devoutly wished for, if not in the immediate future then in the longer term. This is one of the sources of O'Connor's hope for the eventual communion between all human beings, black and white, despite overwhelming evidence that such communion might never be possible.

O'Connor provides a glimpse of such convergence in her novel *The Violent Bear It Away*. The book tells the story of young Francis Tarwater, great-grandnephew of charismatic preacher and Old Testament–style prophet Mason Tarwater, who is freshly dead at the beginning of the novel. Young Tarwater has been marked by his great-uncle—and, as it turns out, by divine power—to be a prophet in the family tradition, and he spends much of the novel running away from his vocation. He does everything he can to deny his identity and evade responsibility, committing outrage after outrage, including the refusal to bury the old man after he dies suddenly at the breakfast table, the attempt to burn his house and his body, the drowning of a child in the course of a botched baptism, and the indulgence in the physical excesses forbidden to him by his great-uncle's ascetic theology. Indeed, Tarwater attempts to ravage every life and landscape he encounters, repeatedly setting his world on fire, both actually and figuratively, in order to destroy it. However, despite his efforts, his destiny cannot be denied, and Tarwater ends up back at the home he ran away from, having endured outrages committed against himself (including homosexual rape), with a new knowledge of who he is and what he is meant for.

In the midst of Tarwater's tale, one figure looms large, that of Buford Munson, a local African American man, with whom the novel begins and ends:

> Francis Marion Tarwater's uncle had been dead for only half a day when the boy got too drunk to finish digging his grave and a Negro named Buford Munson, who had come to get a jug filled, had to finish it and drag the body from the breakfast table where it was still sitting and bury it in a decent and Christian way, with the sign of its Savior at the head of the grave and enough dirt on top to keep the dogs from digging it up. (3)

The opening sentence of the novel immediately grounds us in the moral dimension of Tarwater's universe and demonstrates the ways in which he is living in violation of it. The single steady presence in Tarwater's life after the death of his great-uncle is a black man, introduced not only with a first but also a last name, investing him with an identity and a dignity that are not adjunctive in any way to the white people he lives among. Buford is morally upright, a just man justicing (to paraphrase one of O'Connor's favorite poets, Gerard Manley Hopkins), doing the work Christians are called to do, the Corporal Works of Mercy—the very work young Tarwater refuses.

As Richard Giannone points out in his analysis of the novel, Buford toils from noon to sundown to finish the grave Tarwater abandons in "a work of mercy that is freely given and unassuming," and from his selflessness "there flows an outpouring of spirit that spreads into a Eucharistic vision at the end of the novel" (121). Indeed, Tarwater incurs a debt to Buford, and perhaps on account of that debt, he treats him execrably: "I'm in charge here now and I don't want no nigger-mourning" he tells Buford and his wife as they respond in grief to the old man's death (43), and "Nigger . . . take your hand off me" he says to Buford as the man tries to help the boy up from his drunken stupor, "Go on and lea' me to my bidnis" (48). The boy's scorn is palpable and wounding, at least for the reader, while Buford remains imperturbable, expecting such behavior from a young man who refuses even to bury his own dead. Buford, in his wisdom, foresees the painful pilgrimage the boy is about to embark on: "Nobody going to bother you," he predicts, "That going to be your trouble" (48). That night, after setting fire to the house, young Tarwater heads off to the city in search of his only living relative. Along the way, he accepts a ride from a travelling salesman named Meeks who assures him he is right to be making his escape from the demands of the dead: "That's the way it ought to be in this world—nobody owing nobody nothing" (51).

When Tarwater returns home at the end of the novel, he is much chastened and much changed by the experiences he has undergone. Expecting to find the place totally destroyed by the fires he set upon leaving, he is amazed to behold a vision of a land restored to its former fecundity: "The corn the old man had left planted was up about a foot and moved in wavering lines of green across the field. It had been freshly plowed" (238). This image of life, flourishing beside the blackened chimneys and ruins of the house he abandoned, opens his eyes to a desecrated landscape that has been redeemed. The mundane world seems pervaded by mystery too deep for him to understand. Shortly thereafter, he receives a second vision:

> He saw a Negro mounted on a mule. The mule was not moving; the two might have been made out of rock. He started forward across the field boldly, raising his fist in a gesture that was half-greeting and half-threat, but after a second his hand opened. He waved and began to run. It was Buford. He would go home with him and eat. (239)

Seated astride a donkey, like Christ in the palm procession, Buford waits, monumental, unwavering in his steadfast devotion to the farm Tarwater left behind. Composed of rock, elemental earth, he is the antithesis of the boy who runs, like the element that runs through his name. In addition, he shares a lineage with Saint Peter, whose name means "rock," and upon whom Christ famously founded his Church. Thus, in these twin images, Buford is cast as both redeemer and disciple, and the boy instantly recognizes his authority and runs open-handed toward his saving presence.

Tarwater comes back hungry, insatiable for food that can satisfy—Buford represents the hope of such food and offers the promise of Eucharist as well as the hope of home, a place where he can rest and belong again.

Shortly thereafter, Tarwater sees the grave of his great-uncle Buford has made, the cross Buford placed at the head, and in an extraordinary image, his vision penetrates the surface of the earth so that he perceives the world beneath where the cross's "roots encircled all the dead" (240). In her essay "Asceticism and Abundance: The Communion of Saints in *The Violent Bear It Away*," Susan Srigley connects this image with O'Connor's depiction in *Mystery and Manners* of the action of charity, which "grows invisibly among us, entwining the living and the dead, and is called by the Church the Communion of Saints" ("Asceticism and Abundance" 187; *MM* 228). From this moment, the boy begins to understand, in Srigley's terms, "the relation between life and death, or, more precisely, the relationships between the living and the dead and the spiritual ties that bind them" (186). Before this revelation, Tarwater had resisted "the pull toward communal responsibility," choosing, instead, "to fulfill his individual desires" (188). In keeping with this idea, the boy perceives that, in contrast to Meeks's false assurance and his own preference, he owes the dead—and the living—not less than everything, bound together as we all are in one holy Communion. At the sight of the grave, Tarwater finally relinquishes his willful resistance to his obligations to his fellow communicants, a moment of epiphany signaled by an extraordinary and moving image of release: "The boy's hands opened stiffly as if he were dropping something he had been clutching all his life" (240).

In addition to being the agent of Tarwater's conversion by means of his actions and example, Buford verbally lessons the boy on these theological and moral truths, and does so by deliberately and repeatedly invoking the language of debt: "It's owing to me he's resting there. I buried him while you were laid out drunk. It's owing to me his corn has been plowed. It's owing to me the sign of his Saviour is over his head" (240). The image of a black savior enumerating to a white man the debts he "owes" him is powerful and iconic. The dignity of Buford's speech, which gathers strength with each anaphoric repetition, is matched by the dignity of his bearing. Seated atop his donkey, Buford is taller than the boy and talks down to him from a height that is both physical and spiritual. Buford possesses power, authenticity, and authority—all of which Tarwater lacks. He schools the boy in the ways of being human and holy, speaking to him without fear and without guile. This is no pantomime, no mannered exchange between black and white unequals. In fact, if anyone is lesser than anyone else in human terms, it is the white man.

Though the scene, primarily, has resonance in the context of the story, it also has resonance in the larger realm of racial relations. This is communion—two human beings brought into genuine communication with one another about matters of life and death, redemption and judgment, first things and last. It is no accident that Buford's presence opens the boy up to a final Eucharistic vision, "the field the Negro had crossed ... no longer empty but peopled with a multitude," all of them eating "from a single basket" (241).

This is a version of Teilhard's vision, the long-suffering Buford as stand-in for the crucified Christ, himself divinized, the ravaged land restored and bountiful, the dead man buried and then resurrected in the vision the boy receives, along with all the rest of the dead and the living, too. This vastness of vision imparts a mythic quality to O'Connor's tale, setting this story apart, in some ways, from the more seemingly mundane tales of failed communion mentioned earlier. It is as if the interaction between Buford and Tarwater takes place outside of the context of time and place, local circumstance and condition. At the same time, the conclusion might be seen as a meditation on the problem of race relations in the South and in America as a whole. Buford's repetition of the phrase, "it's owing to me" speaks of spiritual debt, aligning it with the debt human beings owe to Christ for their redemption, but it also speaks of historical, social, and economic debt—the debt white people owe to black people for the sin of slavery, for having kidnapped them and subjected them to servitude, for having stolen their lives and profited from their bodies. Buford's lesson is one for O'Connor's time and one for ours as well. The steady, unacknowledged, uncompensated presence and labor of African Americans has shaped America and Americans (as Toni Morrison argues), and only recently have white people have been called to account. This calling has taken many forms over the decades, articulated by outspoken African American writers, such as W. E. B. Du Bois and his generation, by civil rights leaders and activists, such as James Baldwin and Martin Luther King, by the Black Power movement, including the voice of Malcolm X, and, beyond O'Connor's lifetime and in our own, the calling for reparations for the descendants of enslaved African Americans. Buford Munson schools not just Francis Tarwater—he schools all Americans, he schools the reader (especially the white reader), and he schools O'Connor herself, as she tacitly acknowledges the debt she owes to her fellow human beings, all of whom belong to the Communion of Saints. Buford Munson communes and communicates plainly with Tarwater and with the reader. He dons no protective mask and performs no signifying role. As is typical of O'Connor in portraying black characters in her stories, she makes no attempt to get inside Buford's head, as she does with Tarwater, but she doesn't need to. Munson is transparent, unlike O'Connor's African American characters, who must dissemble for their own safety or who seethe with unspeakable anger. He speaks as one human being to another, creating communion, and inviting us into communion as well.

As was noted earlier, O'Connor prepares the reader—and Tarwater—for this powerful experience of communion in various ways, from the opening of the novel onward. One particular scene that foreshadows Buford's and Tarwater's convergence depicts a fleeting moment of communion between Tarwater and another African American character. During the course of his journey home, Tarwater encounters "a Negro's shack" and "a cluster of colored children watching him from the shack door" (222). Exhausted and thirsty, Tarwater announces "I want me some water," and one of the children, a young black boy who eerily reminds Tarwater of Bishop, the child he drowned in the process of trying to baptize him, points him in the direction of a well beneath a sugarberry tree. In his wandering through this spiritual desert in his quest to return home, Tarwater has unwittingly stumbled upon an oasis. In exchange for water—always a symbol of life—Tarwater gives the child a sandwich from his pocket, a sandwich the child eats immediately, for he is as hungry as Tarwater is thirsty. As if sensing a mysterious connection with the traveler, the child "never removed his eyes from the boy's face" (223). This moment of recognition and of communion—the exchange of life-sustaining food and water—between the two is brief. As Tarwater drinks from the bucket and immerses his head beneath the water, he is shocked by the vision of "two silent serene eyes" gazing at him from the depths. Suddenly the boy feels himself watched and lovingly beheld—by the child he drowned, by the child holding the sandwich, by "the little Negroes" within the shack who "watched him until he was off the place and had disappeared down the highway" (223). Instead of lingering in this *locus amoenus*, a place of safety and refuge, Tarwater does what he consistently does: He runs. He is deeply perturbed by the image of those all-seeing eyes, which he cannot shake. He also realizes that the water "had strangely not assuaged his thirst" (223). Although he does not yet know it, what Tarwater thirsts for is not ordinary water but the "living water" Christ offers the Samaritan woman at the well (John 4:10), just as the bread he hungers for is the bread offered in the novel's final vision of the Eucharistic feast. This early instance of communion with the child, then, might be seen as authentic but incomplete, a harbinger of the fuller communion with Buford that is to come, just as surely as the final Eucharistic vision he receives is but a glimpse of the eternal communion promised in the *Parousia*.

The convergence of blacks and whites in *The Violent Bear It Away* is, ultimately, life-giving, revelatory, and transformative for members of both races. The African American child receives bread and the sudden knowledge of his kinship with the white boy who wanders into his yard, and the white boy receives water and a glimpse of the mystery of his relationship to the child. Buford Munson is able to assert his agency and communicate to Tarwater the debt the young man owes to him and to all the living and the dead, and Tarwater is able to receive the grace offered to him and to see himself and all others in the light of God's mercy. These moments of communion are just that—moments—and are not meant to last, yet they hold out a promise that is rare in O'Connor's writing, extending further the range of possibility in her portrayal of race and race relations in her work. Sometimes, to quote Benito Cereno's words, "the negro" does not signify darkness but, instead, despite America's bleak history, can serve as a conduit of light.

## Two Minds

> Free will does not mean one will, but many wills conflicting in one man.
> 
> Flannery O'Connor, Author's Note to the Second Edition, *Wise Blood*

A concluding, though by no means conclusive, word might be helpful to enable us to summarize the effects of O'Connor's self-described condition of radical ambivalence, her being "of two minds"—perhaps, more precisely, many minds—with regard to race on her writing.

As we have seen in the course of this study, Flannery O'Connor is inconsistent in her treatment of race and depiction of racial relationships in her stories. As we have seen, there is also even greater inconsistency between her attitudes toward race expressed in her letters and those expressed in her fiction. We have seen that she writes differently about race in a letter than she does in a story, that what she writes about race in a letter depends on who she is writing to and what the nature of their correspondence is, and that she sometimes changes her mind about questions having to do with race and then sometimes changes it back again.

We have seen that O'Connor was, in many ways, a product of her culture, that her ideas about race as expressed in her letters were not socially or politically progressive. We have seen that in her letters she sometimes let loose and wrote things she may have wished she didn't. Likely she subscribed to the idea of equality between the races, but it seems she sometimes had a hard time believing it was true, particularly when it came to dealing with individual human beings. We have also seen that in her stories her better angel ruled, that she worked hard at representing the relationship between the races justly, trying not to let her personal feelings and antipathies intervene. We have also seen that her whiteness sometimes prevented her from doing so.

We have seen that O'Connor was transgressive in her writing about race, both in her letters and in her stories, though in different ways. What her art afforded her, and her letters could not, through the twin agencies of sympathetic imagination and fictive discourse, was a means of pushing back against the prejudices she had been privy to her whole life and had, to an extent, internalized. O'Connor's goal was always the truth and "the real" (*MM* 171). She could not varnish, and she would not sugarcoat. We have seen that when she makes fun of racists who despise black people in her stories, she is making fun of herself. We have seen that when she makes fun of liberals who want to ingratiate themselves with black people in her stories, she is making fun of herself. And we have seen that when she depicts black people, who may seem on the surface to be the Other, she is depicting some aspect of herself. As Toni Morrison reminds us, "The subject of the dream is the dreamer" (*Playing in the Dark* 17).

Judging from her letters and most of her fiction, O'Connor did not believe in the practical possibility of communion between whites and blacks on this side of the *Parousia*. She had difficulty conceiving of a world wherein African Americans could function beside white Americans in an equal capacity, perhaps because she had never seen such a world. She ridiculed people who tried to achieve communion between the races in the here and now, including James Baldwin, Martin Luther King Jr., and her friend Maryat Lee. And yet, as we have seen, she pursued this theme over and over in her fiction, from "The Geranium" through "Judgement Day," her first story to her last. Except for the extraordinary moment of communion between Buford Munson and Francis Tarwater and its correlative moment between Tarwater and the black child that foreshadows it, she did not succeed in creating the vision that she continued to hope for, despite her own doubts. The truth, as she saw it, kept breaking in.

These inconsistencies and equivocations are the literary incarnation of O'Connor's uncertainty about the great question of her era, and they also serve as testament to her urgent need to pursue a satisfying answer to this intractable question. This tireless pursuit, in fact, is the source of O'Connor's power as a truth-seeker and her brilliance as a writer. In her author's note to the second edition of *Wise Blood*, O'Connor asserts that the integrity of her protagonist, Hazel Motes, lies in his inability to escape the God who haunts him. She proves the truth of that surprising statement by posing a provocative question and suggesting an answer: "Does one's integrity lie in what he is not able to do? I think that usually it does, for free will does not mean one will, but many wills conflicting in one man" (1).

O'Connor knew firsthand what it meant to harbor many wills conflicting within oneself. Race-haunted as well as God-haunted, O'Connor was pursued by this subject as much as she pursued it, and, like Hazel, she could not escape its powerful pull. In writing about race, she struggled against her inclinations, fought with friends and family, and vigorously engaged radically opposing ideas. She held in tension her "two minds"—and more—and out of that quarrel within herself (to echo Yeats's terms), created a complex poetry that embodies her ambivalence. By her own definition, O'Connor's integrity as an artist lies, like Hazel's, in what she was not able to do, as well as in what she was. Flannery O'Connor may not have fully achieved the belief in and the vision of racial communion that she pursued and that hotly pursued her, but, like her obsessed and relentless protagonist, she lived and died trying.

Acknowledgments

Every project has an origin. The idea for a book sometimes arrives like a sudden thunderbolt, while at other times it arrives gradually by means of a long slow burn. *Radical Ambivalence* came about as a result of the latter process. I have been reading, writing about, and teaching Flannery O'Connor's fiction, essays, and correspondence for many years. With this deepening of my acquaintance with O'Connor and her work, my understanding of her work has evolved over the years in a number of ways. One constant preoccupation throughout this process of evolution has been my growing discomfort with O'Connor's treatment of race. For a long time, I adopted the position that many O'Connor scholars held and hold to—that she was somehow immune from the racism of her culture and era and that she consciously challenged racist views of African Americans in her stories. However, even as I laid claim to these convictions, I felt dissatisfaction with that critical consensus. Her portrayal of African American characters in stories such as "Everything that Rises Must Converge," "The Artificial Nigger," and "Judgement Day" troubled me in ways I didn't think they were intended to. I couldn't quite put my finger on what disturbed me about them, but I felt it when I read the stories, when I taught them to my students, and when I discussed them in the context of faculty seminars with scholars from other disciplines who were less familiar with O'Connor's work. These readers, young and old, spoke of an unsettling element in O'Connor's vision, a blind spot when it came to race, that I myself sensed but could not articulate in a satisfying way. This book has given me the opportunity to do that—to pursue the questions that have nagged me (and others) and discover ways to talk about O'Connor's treatment of race that illuminates the stories, the writer, and the expectations of our own era of writers who deal with this topic that is so essential to us as Americans living in the current post–civil rights, Black Lives Matter historical moment.

I approach this subject with enthusiasm and also with humility. As a white person exploring the portrayal of race in O'Connor, I have tried to be aware of the ways in which my racial orientation inevitably limits my perspective. To help remedy this, I have depended upon the perspectives of African American writers and scholars, including Toni Morrison, Alice Walker, James Baldwin, Ralph Ellison, Hilton Als, M. Shawn Copeland, Bryan Massingale, and others. It is my hope that these writers' nuanced and more penetrating visions with regard to the issue of race have enlarged and deepened my own.

This is the first of many debts I owe. It is a commonplace that all biographers and literary scholars stand on the shoulders of those who have come before them, and this is certainly true of my experience in writing this book. This first book-length study of O'Connor's treatment of race builds on a rich body of existing work in this area of O'Connor scholarship, and it is my hope that it will advance and deepen that conversation as well as fuel future studies. A quick glance at the bibliography indicates the number of writers and scholars I have relied on for insight, for information, and for inspiration.

I am grateful, foremost, to Sally Fitzgerald for her foundational work in editing O'Connor's letters, which have enabled several generations of scholars to hear O'Connor tell the story of her life and relay her most private thoughts in her own inimitable voice. *The Habit of Being* has been my constant companion throughout this project, second only to my copy of O'Connor's *Complete Stories*, as a text I have read from each day and relied upon to ground the study in O'Connor's words.

In addition, I want to express my gratitude to the great Flannery O'Connor scholars who have taught me how to read her fiction, correspondence, and critical essays, including critics whose work I have recently discovered, such as Doreen Fowler and Susan Srigley, as well as those whose books I have been reading and rereading over my many years of teaching, studying, and writing about O'Connor, especially Ralph Wood and Richard Giannone. I also owe a debt of gratitude to O'Connor's biographers, especially Paul Elie and Brad Gooch, who in frankly addressing the question of race in O'Connor's work confirmed my own discomfort and encouraged me to pursue this study.

I would not have been able to complete this project without the assistance of the good people at the Special Collections at Georgia College and

State University, where O'Connor's letters, manuscripts, and memorabilia are housed. My special thanks go to Nancy Davis-Bray, Associate Director for Special Collections, for her hours of attention while I was perusing the letters exchanged between Flannery O'Connor and Maryat Lee. In addition, I am grateful to have received an Ina Dillard Russell Library Research Grant to travel to Milledgeville to conduct my research. My thanks also go to the archivists at the Stuart A. Rose Manuscript, Archives, & Rare Book Library at Emory University, especially Kathy Shoemaker, for their assistance during my visit to view the letters exchanged between Flannery O'Connor and Elizabeth Hester and those exchanged between Flannery and Maryat Lee.

With regard to the materials I examined at these archives, I am grateful to Louise Florencourt, cousin to Flannery O'Connor, and Fr. Michael Garanzini, joint trustees of the Mary Flannery O'Connor Trust, for permission to quote from these previously unpublished letters. They are an invaluable resource in clarifying O'Connor's complex attitudes about race, and giving scholars like myself permission to publicize them promotes a fuller understanding of O'Connor's work and opens up exciting possibilities for future discussion.

I want to express my deep gratitude to the friends, colleagues, and mentors who have read and commented on this manuscript, especially Joseph Viscomi, Richard Giannone, Susan Srigley, Joseph Flora, and Heidi Kim. Thanks to their belief in the project and generous contributions of time and expertise, this is a better and a richer book.

I am also grateful to my colleagues Christine Firer Hinze and Maria Terzulli, whom I am fortunate to work with at Fordham University's Curran Center for American Catholic Studies, for their support and encouragement throughout this project. Their willingness to carry an extra burden made it possible for me to complete the book. In this, as in many other ways, their generosity abounds.

As ever, I am grateful to my family. My three sons, Charles, Patrick, and William, grew up in Baltimore, Maryland, a city with a long history of racial division and unrest. Spending their childhood and young adulthood bearing witness to the many forms of racism deeply engrained in the culture of their hometown opened their eyes to the injustice African Americans endure and motivated them to pursue work that attempts to redress that injustice. These young men inspire me every day.

Finally, I am grateful to my husband, Brennan, for his friendship and support in this, as in so many literary projects. We discovered Flannery O'Connor together as undergraduates and fell in love with her work. As fellow academics and professors, we have read and taught O'Connor's stories for decades. She has been the topic of conversation at so many of our family meals, she may as well have been there with us. His willingness to read and offer advice on yet another of my projects devoted to her work is a sign of his love, for which I am most grateful of all.

Grateful acknowledgment is made to the following publishers and holders of copyright for permission to quote from and/or reprint copyrighted material:

Farrar, Straus and Giroux, LLC: Excerpts from *The Complete Stories* by Flannery O'Connor. Copyright © 1971 by the Estate of Mary Flannery O'Connor. Excerpts from *The Habit of Being: Letters of Flannery O'Connor*, edited by Sally Fitzgerald. Copyright © 1979 by Regina O'Connor. Excerpts from *Mystery and Manners* by Flannery O'Connor. Copyright © 1969 by the Estate of Mary Flannery O'Connor. Excerpts from *The Violent Bear It Away* by Flannery O'Connor. Copyright © 1960 by Flannery O'Connor. Copyright renewed 1988 by Regina O'Connor. Excerpts from *A Prayer Journal*. Copyright © 2013 by Mary Flannery O'Connor Charitable Trust.

Harold Matson Co., Inc.: Excerpts from *The Complete Stories* by Flannery O'Connor. Copyright © 1971 by the Estate of Mary Flannery O'Connor. Excerpts from *The Habit of Being: Letters of Flannery O'Connor*, edited by Sally Fitzgerald. Copyright © 1979 by Regina O'Connor. Excerpts from *Mystery and Manners* by Flannery O'Connor. Copyright © 1969 by the Estate of Mary Flannery O'Connor. Excerpts from *A Prayer Journal*. Copyright © 2013 by Mary Flannery O'Connor Charitable Trust.

Excerpts from unpublished letters are reprinted by permission of Mary Flannery O'Connor Charitable Trust via Harold Matson Co., Inc. © 1962, 1964 Flannery O'Connor; © renewed by Regina Cline O'Connor. All rights reserved.

# Works cited

## Works by Flannery O'Connor

O'Connor, Flannery. Author's Note to the Second Edition. *Wise Blood.* New York: Farrar, Straus & Giroux, 2007, 1.

———. "The Coat." *DoubleTake* 2.3 (1996): 38–41.

———. *The Complete Stories.* New York: Farrar, Straus & Giroux, 1971.

———. *Flannery O'Connor: Collected Works.* Ed. Sally Fitzgerald. New York: Library of America, 1988.

———. *The Habit of Being: Letters of Flannery O'Connor.* Ed. Sally Fitzgerald. New York: Farrar, Straus & Giroux, 1979.

———. *Mystery & Manners.* Ed. Sally Fitzgerald and Robert Fitzgerald. New York: Farrar, Straus & Giroux, 1970.

———. *A Prayer Journal.* Ed. William Sessions. New York: Farrar, Straus & Giroux, 2015.

———. *The Violent Bear It Away.* New York: Farrar, Straus & Giroux, 2007.

## Unpublished Letters and Excerpts from Letters

Flannery O'Connor. Letter to Elizabeth Ames. 17 August 1948. O'Connor Guest File. Yaddo, Saratoga Springs, NY.

Flannery O'Connor. Letter to Elizabeth Hester. 27 June 1964. Flannery O'Connor Letters. Stuart A. Rose Manuscript, Archives, and Rare Book Library. Emory University, Atlanta, GA.

Flannery O'Connor. Letter to Maryat Lee. 3 May 1964. Flannery O'Connor Collection. Ina Dillard Russell Library. Georgia College and State University, Milledgeville, GA.

Flannery O'Connor. Letter to Maryat Lee. 21 May 1962. Flannery O'Connor Collection. Ina Dillard Russell Library. Georgia College and State University, Milledgeville, GA.

Flannery O'Connor. Letter to Maryat Lee. 17 November 1962. Flannery O'Connor Letters. Stuart A. Rose Manuscript, Archives, and Rare Book Library. Emory University, Atlanta, GA.

Primary and Critical Sources

Alexander, Benjamin D. "These Jesuits Work Fast: O'Connor's Elusive Politics." *A Political Companion to Flannery O'Connor*. Ed. Henry T. Edmonson III. Lexington: University of Kentucky Press, 2017, 45–67.

Allen, Theodore. *The Invention of the White Race, Vol. 2: The Origin of Racial Oppression in Anglo-America*. New York: Verso, 1997.

Als, Hilton. "This Lonesome Place: Flannery O'Connor on Race and Religion in the Unreconstructed South." *White Girls*. San Francisco: McSweeney's, 2013, 111–31.

Armstrong, Julie. "Blinded by Whiteness: Revisiting Flannery O'Connor and Race." *The Flannery O'Connor Review* 1 (2001–2002): 77–87.

Asals, Frederick. *Flannery O'Connor: The Imagination of Extremity*. Athens: University of Georgia Press, 1982.

Babb, Valerie. *Whiteness Visible: The Meaning of Whiteness in American Literature and Culture*. New York: New York University Press, 1998.

Baldwin, James. *The Fire Next Time*. New York: Vintage, 1993.

———. *I Am Not Your Negro*. Ed. Raoul Peck. New York: Vintage, 2017.

———. "They Can't Turn Back." *Collected Essays*. New York: Library of America, 1998, 622–37.

Blanding, Michael. *The Coke Machine: The Dirty Truth Behind the World's Favorite Soft Drink*. New York: Avery, 2010.

Brinkmeyer, Robert. *The Art and Vision of Flannery O'Connor*. Baton Rouge: Louisiana State University Press, 1989.

Caron, Timothy P. "'The Bottom Rail Is on Top': Race and 'Theological Whiteness' in Flannery O'Connor's Short Fiction." *Inside the Church of Flannery O'Connor*. Eds. Joanna Halleran McMullen and Jon Parrish Peede. Macon, GA: Mercer University Press, 2007, 138–64.

Cash, Jean W. *Flannery O'Connor*. Knoxville: University of Tennessee Press, 2002.

———. "'Maryat and Flanneryat': An Antithetical Friendship." *The Flannery O'Connor Bulletin* 19 (1990): 56–73.

Clerc, Charles. "Anatomy of Welty's 'Where Is the Voice Coming From?'" *Studies in Short Fiction* 23 (1986): 389–400.

Cohen, Leonard. "Anthem." *The Future*. Columbia, 1992.

Copeland, M. Shawn. *Enfleshing Freedom: Body, Race, and Being*. Minneapolis: Fortress Press, 2010.

Crawford, Nicholas. "An Africanist Impasse: Race, Return, and Revelation in the Fiction of Flannery O'Connor." *South Atlantic Review* 68.2 (Spring 2003): 1–25.

Davis, Cyprian. *The History of Black Catholics in the United States*. New York: Crossroad, 1991.

Day, Matthew. "Flannery O'Connor and the Southern Code of Manners." *Southern Crossroads: Perspectives on Religion and Culture*. Eds. Walter H. Conser Jr. and Rodger M. Payne. Lexington: University of Kentucky Press, 2008, 133–44.

Delgado, Richard, and Jean Stefancic. *Critical Race Theory*, 3rd ed. New York: New York University Press, 2017.

Douglas, Mary. *Natural Symbols: Explorations in Cosmology*, 2nd ed. New York: Routledge, 1996.

Du Bois, W. E. B. *The Souls of Black Folk*. New York: Norton, 1999.

———. "The Souls of White Folk." *Darkwater: Voices from within the Veil*. New York: Harcourt, Brace, & Company, 1920, 30–34.

Dunleavy, Janet Egleson. "A Particular History: Black and White in Flannery O'Connor's Short Fiction." *Critical Essays on Flannery O'Connor*. Eds. Melvin J. Friedman and Beverly Lyon Clark. Boston: Hall, 1985, 186–202.

Duvall, John N. *Race and White Identity in Southern Fiction: From Faulkner to Morrison*. New York: Palgrave Macmillan, 2012.

Elie, Paul. *The Life You Save May Be Your Own: An American Pilgrimage*. New York: Farrar, Straus & Giroux, 2003.

Ellison, Ralph. *Invisible Man*. New York: Random House, 1994.

———. *Shadow and Act*. New York: Random House, 1953.

Fitzgerald, Robert. Introduction. *Everything That Rises Must Converge*. New York: Macmillan, 1965, vii–xxxiv.

Fowler, Doreen. "Aligning the Psychological with the Theological: Doubling and Race in Flannery O'Connor's Fiction." *The Flannery O'Connor Review* 13 (2015): 78–89.

———."Deconstructing Racial Difference: Flannery O'Connor's 'The Artificial Nigger.'" *The Flannery O'Connor Bulletin* 24 (1995–96): 22–32.

———. "Writing and Rewriting Race: Flannery O'Connor's 'The Geranium' and 'Judgement Day.'" *The Flannery O'Connor Review* 2 (2003-4): 31–39.

Frankenberg, Ruth. *White Women, Race Matters: The Social Construction of Whiteness*. Minneapolis: University of Minnesota Press, 1993.

Gates, Henry Louis, Jr. *Signifying Monkey: A Theory of African American Literary Criticism*. New York: Oxford University Press, 2004.

Giannone, Richard. *Flannery O'Connor and the Mystery of Love*. Champaign: University of Illinois Press, 1989.

Gooch, Brad. *Flannery: A Life*. New York: Little Brown & Company, 2009.

Gordon, Sarah. *Flannery O'Connor: The Obedient Imagination*. Athens: University of Georgia Press, 2000.

Gossett, Thomas F. *Race: The History of an Idea in America*. New York: Schocken, 1965.

Hale, Grace Elizabeth. *Making Whiteness: The Culture of Segregation in the South, 1890–1940*. New York: Vintage, 1999.

Harris, Carole K. "On Flying Mules and the Southern Cabala: Flannery O'Connor and James Baldwin in Georgia." *Renascence: Essays on Values in*

*Literature*, 22 September 2013: 1–18. The Free Library, www.thefreelibrary.com/On+flying+mules+and+the+Southern+cabala%3A+Flannery+O%27Connor+and+James . . . -a0353645258.

*Holy Bible*. New International Version. Grand Rapids, MI: Zondervan, 2015.

Kahane, Claire. "The Artificial Niggers." *The Massachusetts Review* 29.1 (1978): 183–98.

Kennedy, Randall. *Nigger: The Strange Career of a Troublesome Word*. New York: Vintage, 2003.

King, Thomas. Introduction. *The Divine Milieu* by Teilhard de Chardin. Portland, OR: Sussex Academic Press, 2004.

Locke, Alain. *The New Negro*. Eastford, CT: Martino Fine Books, 2015.

Lynch, William. *Christ and Apollo: The Dimensions of the Literary Imagination*. New York: Mentor-Omega, 1963.

Mackethan, Lucinda H. "Redeeming Blackness: Urban Allegories of O'Connor, Percy, and Toole." *Studies in the Literary Imagination* 27.2 (1994): 29–39.

MacMullan, Terrance. "Facing up to Ignorance and Privilege: Philosophy of Whiteness as Public Intellectualism." *Philosophy Compass* 10.9 (2015), 646–60. Wiley Online Library, 10.1111/phc3.12238. Doi 10.1111/phc3.12238/full.

Magee, Rosemary. *Conversations with Flannery O'Connor*. Jackson: University Press of Mississippi, 1987.

Massingale, Bryan N. "Has the Silence Been Broken? Catholic Theological Ethics and Racial Justice." *Theological Studies* 75.1 (2014), 133–55.

———. *Racial Justice and the Catholic Church*. Maryknoll, NY: Orbis Books, 2017.

McCown, James Hart. *With Crooked Lines*. Mobile, AL: Spring Hill College Press, 1990.

Melville, Herman. "Benito Cereno." *The Piazza Tales and Other Prose Pieces, 1839–1860*. Evanston, IL: Northwestern University Press, 1987, 46–117.

———. "Hawthorne and His Mosses." *The Piazza Tales and Other Prose Pieces, 1839–1860*. Evanston, IL: Northwestern University Press, 1987, 239–53.

Meriwether, James B., and Michael Millgate, eds. *Lion in the Garden: Interviews with William Faulkner, 1926–1962*. New York: Random House, 1968.

Morrison, Toni. *Beloved*. New York: Vintage, 2004.

———. *Playing in the Dark: Whiteness and the Literary Imagination*. Cambridge, MA: Harvard University Press, 1992.

Nesbitt, Laurel. "Reading Place in and around O'Connor's Texts." *Post Identity* 1.1 (Fall 1997): 1–30. MPublishing, University of Michigan Library, quod.lib.umich.edu/p/postid/pid9999.0001.107/--reading-place-in-and-around-flannery-oconnors-texts?rgn=main;view=fulltext.

Omi, Michael, and Howard Winant. *Racial Formation in the United States: From the 1960s to the 1980s*. New York: Routledge, 1986.

———. *Racial Formation in the United States: From the 1960s to the 1990s*, 2nd ed. New York: Routledge, 1994.

Osborne, William A. *The Segregated Covenant: Race Relations and American Catholics*. New York: Herder and Herder, 1967.

Percy, Walker. *Signposts in a Strange Land*. New York: Picador, 2000.
——. "Stoicism in the South." *The Commonweal* LXIV (July 6, 1956): 342–44.
Perreault, Jeanne. "The Body, the Critics, and 'The Artificial Nigger.'" *The Mississippi Quarterly* 56.3 (Summer 2003): 389–411.
Polk, Noel. "Faulkner and the White Southern Moderate." *Faulkner and Race: Faulkner and Yoknapatawpha, 1986*. Eds. Doreen Fowler and Ann J. Abadie. Jackson: University of Mississippi Press, 1987, 130–51.
Pollack, Harriet. "Reading Welty of Whiteness and Race." *Eudora Welty, Whiteness, and Race*. Ed. Harriet Pollack. Athens: University of Georgia Press, 2013, 1–22.
Roberts, Diane. *The Myth of Aunt Jemima: Representations of Race and Region*. New York: Routledge, 1994.
Schroeder, Michael L. "Desegregation and the Silent Character in 'Everything That Rises Must Converge.'" *A Political Companion to Flannery O'Connor*. Ed. Henry T. Edmonson III. Lexington: University of Kentucky Press, 2017, 68–78.
Sessions, William. Introduction. *A Prayer Journal* by Flannery O'Connor. New York: Farrar, Straus & Giroux, 2015, vii–xii.
Shackleford, Dean D. "The Black Outsider in O'Connor's Fiction." *The Flannery O'Connor Bulletin* 18 (1989): 79–90.
Shakespeare, William. *Hamlet*. In *The Riverside Shakespeare*. Ed. G. Blakemore Evans. Boston: Houghton Mifflin, 1974, 1135–97.
——. *Romeo and Juliet*. In Evans, *The Riverside Shakespeare*, 1055–99.
Smith, Barbara Herrnstein. *On the Margins of Discourse*. Chicago: University of Chicago Press, 1979.
Srigley, Susan. "Asceticism and Abundance: The Communion of Saints in *The Violent Bear It Away*." *Dark Faith: New Essays on Flannery O'Connor's The Violent Bear It Away*. Ed. Susan Srigley. South Bend, IN: University of Notre Dame Press, 2012, 185–212.
Stern, Richard. "Flannery O'Connor: A Remembrance and Some Letters." *Shenandoah* 16 (1965): 5–10.
Styron, William. "This Quiet Dust." *Voices in Our Blood: America's Best on the Civil Rights Movement*. Ed. John Meacham. New York: Random House, 2001, 328–45.
Sullivan, Shannon. *Revealing Whiteness: The Unconscious Habits of Racial Privilege*. Bloomington: Indiana University Press, 2008.
Sykes, John D. "Flannery O'Connor and the Agrarians: Authentic Religion and Southern Identity." *A Political Companion to Flannery O'Connor*. Ed. Henry T. Edmondson III. Lexington: University Press of Kentucky, 2017, 21–44.
Walker, Alice. "Beyond the Peacock: The Reconstruction of Flannery O'Connor." *In Search of Our Mother's Gardens: Womanist Prose*. New York: Harcourt, Brace, Jovanovich, 1983, 42–59.

Welty, Eudora. "Where Is the Voice Coming From?" *Eudora Welty: Stories, Essays, & Memoir*. Eds. Richard Ford and Michael Krayling. New York: Library of America, 1998, 727–32.

Whitt, Margaret Earley. "The Pivotal Year, 1963: Flannery O'Connor and the Civil Rights Movement." *A Political Companion to Flannery O'Connor*. Ed. Henry T. Edmonson III. Lexington: University of Kentucky Press, 2017, 79–98.

Williams, Melvin G. "Black and White: A Study in Flannery O'Connor's Characters." *Black American Literature Forum* 10.4 (Winter 1976): 130–32.

Wood, Ralph C. *The Comedy of Redemption: Christian Faith and Comic Vision in Four American Novelists*. Notre Dame, IN: Notre Dame University Press, 1988.

———. *Flannery O'Connor and the Christ-Haunted South*. Grand Rapids, MI: Eerdman's, 2005.

———. "Flannery O'Connor's Racial Morals and Manners." *The Christian Century* 111:33 (1994): 1076–82.

———. "From Fashionable Tolerance to Unfashionable Redemption: A Reading of Flannery O'Connor's First and Last Stories." *The Flannery O'Connor Bulletin* 7 (1978): 10–25.

———. "Where Is the Voice Coming From? Flannery O'Connor on Race." *The Flannery O'Connor Bulletin* 22 (1993–1994): 90–118.

Yeats, W. B. "Anima Hominus." *Per Amica Silentia Lunae*. New York: Macmillan, 1918, 17–50.

# Index

Acton, John Emerich Edward, Baron, 73
African Americans: anger of, 32; civil rights movement, 19, 20; construction of a white consciousness and, 10; historical background of, 61; liberation of, 21; performative expectations, 23; southerners' stereotypes about, 62; struggle for survival, 48–49
Alexander, Benjamin, 62
Ali, Muhammad, 52
Als, Hilton, 3
American Africanism, 97, 98
American Catholic Church, 82, 87, 88
American literature: Africanist presence in, 98, 106; Civil War in, 128; question of race in, 97, 125; southern writers, 129; white blindness of, 98–99, 126
Ames, Elizabeth, 76
Armstrong, Julie, 6, 7, 19, 24, 57
"Artificial Nigger, The" (O'Connor): adult/child relationships in, 46; black/white relations in, 67, 110–11, 120; critical studies of, 11, 98, 115; description of the sewers, 114, 122; image of black woman, 104, 113–16; image of statue of Negro, 117–19; image of the train, 118; O'Connor's perception of, 110, 115; plot, 110, 112; publication of, 57; repetition of the word "colored," 112; revelation of sexual mystery, 114; scene of black neighborhood, 112–13; theme of redemption, 117–18

Asbury Fox (character): communion of, 134; encounter with black people, 132, 133–34; homecoming of, 132; illness of, 132, 133; racial tolerance of, 132, 133
Asals, Frederick: *Flannery O'Connor: The Imagination of Extremity*, 118

Babb, Valerie, 34
Baldwin, James, 139, 142; on concept of "nigger," 60, 61; *The Fire Next Time*, 134, 135; O'Connor opinion about, 49–50, 51, 52; on racist code, 44; television interview, 60; "They Can't Turn Back," 22
"Barber, The" (O'Connor): black/white relations in, 43–44, 131; characters of, 41–42, 43–44; critique of, 41–42, 44; plot, 41; treatment of race in, 10
Barnett, Ross, 39
*Benito Cereno* (Melville), 126–27, 130
Birmingham Baptist Church bombing, 36, 37
black Catholics: segregation of, 84
blackness: culture of segregation and, 18, 107; idea of, 16, 126; in O'Connor's fiction, 96, 98, 111, 127; social construction of, 30, 34, 110, 119
Black Power movement, 139
black women's bodies: in Catholic theology, treatment of, 101, 102; as image for social reality, 102; as maternal figure, 114; as sexual object, 102, 114–15, 121–22; slavery and, 101–2, 115; as surrogate body, 120; treatment of, 87–88; violence on, 101

"Blinded by Whiteness: Revisiting
  Flannery O'Connor" (Armstrong), 6
body: social and physical attributes, 102;
  theological concept of, 101. *See also*
  physical body; social body
Breit, Harvey, 12
Bremerwell, Gloria, 40
Brinkmeyer, Robert, 116
*Brown vs. Board of Education*, 15, 40
Buford Munson (character), 136, 137, 138,
  139, 141

Caron, Timothy, 8, 96, 119
Carver (character), 107, 108
Cash, Jean, 47, 49
Cather, Willa: *Sapphira and the Slave Girl*,
  108
Catholic Church: attitudes toward race
  and segregation, 10, 83–85; civil rights
  movement and, 85; historical evolution
  of, 85–86, 88; Jim Crow's influence in, 85;
  participation in slave trade, 83. *See also*
  Second Vatican Council
Chardin, Teilhard de, 80, 135
civil rights movement, 7, 19, 20, 39–40, 81
Civil War: in American literature, 128;
  outcome of, 130; theological perspective
  on, 130
Clay, Cassius. *See* Ali, Muhammad
Coca-Cola: invention of, 129
Coca-Cola machines, 50
Cohen, Leonard, 69
Coleman (character): as Africanist Other,
  120–21; mystical identity of, 26, 32;
  personality of, 28; relationship with
  Tanner, 2, 27, 29, 33; violent behavior of,
  32, 33; vision of reality, 30–31
color-blindness: concept of, 41, 42–43
communion: between all human beings,
  135; between the races, 11, 132, 134–35,
  140, 141, 142; of Saints, 95, 138, 139
Copeland, M. Shawn, 10, 87, 88, 102, 115;
  *Enfleshing Freedom: Body, Race, &
  Being*, 101
Crawford, Nicholas, 4
critical whiteness studies, 7, 11, 16, 18

Davis, Cyprian, 83
Dawkins, Cecil, 76, 90
Day, Dorothy, 82
Day, Matthew, 132
Delgado, Richard, 43
Douglas, Mary, 10, 102

Du Bois, W. E. B., 15, 18, 139
Dudley (character). *See* Old Dudley
  (character)
Dunleavy, Janet Egleson, 7, 47
Duvall, John N.: *Race and White Identity
  in Southern Literature*, 8

Elie, Paul, 4, 53, 76
Ellison, Ralph, 125; *Invisible Man*, 127–28
"Enduring Chill, The" (O'Connor): black/
  white relationships in, 67, 132–33, 134;
  main characters, 41; moments of
  communion, 132; plot, 132
Evers, Medgar, 36, 37, 61
"Everything That Rises Must Converge"
  (O'Connor): black/white relationships, 67,
  104–5, 107–8, 119, 131; depiction of black
  woman, 32, 103–5, 106, 107–8; O'Connor's
  perspective on, 102, 105, 119; parent/child
  relations in, 103, 107, 108; plot, 102–4;
  publication of, 1, 106; title of, 81; white
  characters, 3, 41, 44, 102–3, 105–6

Faulkner, William, 9; *As I Lay Dying*, 73
fictive discourse: *vs.* natural discourse,
  67–68
Fitzgerald, Robert, 73–74
Fitzgerald, Sally: defense of O'Connor's
  racial attitude, 63, 64, 66; discovery of
  "The Coat," 45; friendship with O'Connor,
  73, 74, 75; publication of O'Connor's
  letters, 4, 64, 65
Fowler, Doreen: on adult/child relationship,
  107; studies of O'Connor's fiction, 7, 15,
  16, 25, 33, 41–42, 44, 112
Francis Tarwater (character): conversion
  of, 138; death of uncle, 136; denial of
  responsibility, 136; interaction between
  Buford Munson and, 137, 139, 140;
  moment of communion of, 140; story of,
  135–36; traveling salesman and, 137;
  visions of, 137, 139
Frankenberg, Ruth, 7

General Sash (character), 128–29
George (character), 43–44, 89, 131
Georgia: black/white relations in, 50
"Geranium, The" (O'Connor): black/white
  relationship in, 2, 10, 27, 28, 29, 45, 120;
  characters, 25–26; comic dream in,
  33–34; dialectical relationship of
  characters, 27; explorations of whiteness,
  25; plot, 1, 26–27, 28; revisions of, 1, 2

Giannone, Richard, 33, 80, 136; *Flannery O'Connor and the Mystery of Love*, 25
Giroux, Robert, 25, 73, 74
Gooch, Brad, 53, 65; *Flannery*, 40
Gordon, Sarah, 45, 79
Gossett, Thomas, 61, 62; *Race: The History of an Idea in America*, 61
Grace, Mary (character), 90, 92, 93
Gross, W. H., Bishop of Savannah, 84

Hale, Grace Elizabeth, 17, 23
Harris, Carole K., 22, 51
Hawthorne, Nathaniel: fiction stories of, 126
Hayes, Patrick, Cardinal, 85
Hazel Motes (character), 75, 76, 142
Hester, Elizabeth: O'Connor's letters to, 1, 4, 6, 10, 40, 59, 64–65, 75, 91–92, 96, 100
Hill, Jack, 64
Hill, Louise, 64, 65
Howe, Russell, 9
Hughes, John, Archbishop of New York, 83
Hughes, Philip, 73
Hyland, Francis Edward, Bishop of Atlanta, 85

idolatry, 87–88
*Index Librorum Prohibitorum*, 80
Ireland, John, Bishop of St. Paul, Minnesota, 84
Irish Catholics: clashes with African Americans, 83

Jacobs (character), 41–42, 43
Jim Crow system, 15, 17, 50, 85
"Judgement Day" (O'Connor), 67, 75; Africanist Others in, 120–22; characters, 25–26; depiction of racial relations, 45; explorations of whiteness in, 25; plot, 1–2, 26–27; study of, 10, 11; versions of, 25
Julian (character): description of black woman body, 103–5, 107; encounter with black man, 131, 133; liberal views of, 103; relationship with mother, 102–3
Julian's mother (character): conflict with black woman, 104, 105; death of, 105–6, 107, 108; dream of home, 106; final words of, 106; racist views of, 3, 103; relationships with son, 102–3

Kahane, Claire, 6, 15, 115, 120
Kennedy, John F., 36, 38, 61, 86
Kennedy, Randall: *Nigger: The Strange Career of a Troublesome Word*, 60–61

King, Fr. Thomas, 80
King, Martin Luther, Jr., 36, 52, 61, 85, 139, 142
Ku Klux Klan, 23, 50

Lee, Maryat: background of, 49; friendship with O'Connor, 49, 92–93, 142; nicknames of, 53; O'Connor's letters to, 3, 10, 18–20, 38, 50, 51, 53–55, 64–65, 86, 99; as prototype of Mary Grace, 92; views on race, 49
Lee, Robert E., 49
Locke, Alain, 19
Lowell, Robert, 73
Lynch, William, 10; *Christ and Apollo*, 79
lynching, 21, 23, 63

Macauley, Robie, 73
MacKethan, Lucinda H., 116
MacMullan, Terrance, 42
Manson, Willie, 64
Massingale, Bryan, 10, 87; *Racial Justice and the Catholic Church*, 87
Mayhew, Leonard, 65
McCown, James Hart, 61–62, 64, 80; *God Writes with Crooked Lines*, 62
Melville, Herman, 125, 126, 131; *Benito Cereno*, 126–27
Mitchell, Margaret: influence of, 128
Morrison, Toni: analysis of American literature, 10, 97–99, 106; on black/white relations, 108; critique of O'Connor's fiction, 123, 124, 142; on perception of African American women, 101; *Playing in the Dark*, 10, 15, 66, 97–98, 101, 106, 123, 124; study of whiteness, 66, 126
Mr. Head (character): betrayal of Nelson, 116–17; conversion of, 118; encounter with a black body, 116; horror of black neighborhood, 112–13; perception of black people, 110, 111, 113, 118

natural discourse: *vs.* fictive discourse, 10, 67–68
"Negro": meaning of the word, 127; *vs.* "nigger," 56, 58
Nelson (character): "artificial nigger" and, 117, 118–19; conversion of, 118; encounter with black bodies, 110–11, 112–16, 118; Mr. Head's betrayal of, 116–17; perception of racial differences, 111–12; sexual anxiety of, 114
Nesbitt, Laurel, 119

Newman, John Henry, 73
New York City: draft riots in, 83
"nigger": history of the term, 59, 60–61, 66; vs. "Negro," 56, 58; O'Connor's reference to, 4, 53, 56, 58, 59–60, 65–66; racial connotation of the word, 57
Nipson, Herb, 40

O'Connor, Flannery: analogical vision of, 78, 95; attempt to escape white culture, 48, 96; Catholic influence on, 10, 76–77, 78–79; conversations with Catholic writers, 73–74; conversion of, 96; criticism of African American activists, 52, 53; cultural background of, 10, 38–39, 59, 66; death of father, 77; education of, 71, 72; faith, crisis of, 70, 71–72; friends of, 49, 61, 62, 72–73, 92–93; as godmother to the Fitzgeralds' child, 74; historical era of, 18; identity formation of, 49; illness of, 21, 48, 65, 74–75, 77–78, 99–100; intellectual curiosity of, 80; interviews of, 21; legacy of, 3, 13; life in Georgia, 76; life in Iowa, 40, 45; life in New York City, 72, 73; literary awards, 129; McCown's influence on, 61–62; National Book Award, 15; nicknames of, 53; participation in religious rituals, 71, 73; personality of, 109; political views of, 40; *Prayer Journal* of, 71–72; protection of reputation of, 5; publishing career of, 20; on pursuit of the real, 24; racial attitudes of, 47–49, 51–52, 53, 56, 68, 70; reading preferences, 79–80; relationship to the Church, 77, 82, 86, 88; relationship with mother, 59, 108–9; self-perception of, 11, 12; support of segregation, 19; tension of "two minds" of, 143; theological views of, 38, 68–69, 70, 77–81; tribalism of, 55; white prejudices of, 8; at Yaddo artists' community, 72, 73
O'Connor, Regina Cline: control of estate, 4; personality of, 109; relationships with daughter, 59, 75, 108–9; treatment of black people, 64–65
O'Connor's fiction: adult/child relations in, 107, 109; attention to bodies, 98, 99, 100, 101, 103–5, 123; characters of liberal thought, 41, 44; Civil War in, 128–30; "The Coat," 10, 45, 46–47; *Collected Works*, 4, 55; *Complete Stories*, 15; critical studies of, 6–9, 11, 13–14, 15, 67; depiction of black characters, 6, 8, 13–16, 23, 32–33, 98, 139–40; "The Displaced Person," 67; effect on readers, 123–24; God's grace in, 16; *The Habit of Being*, 4, 5, 55, 65; inconsistencies in, 142; "The Lame Shall Enter First," 41; language and tropes of, 8, 56–58; "A Late Encounter with the Enemy," 128–29; limitations of, 11, 24; *A Memoir of Mary Ann*, 37; mystery in, 79; natural and fictive discourse of, 68; "Parker's Back," 75; popularity of, 12; publishers of, 73; racial issues in, 4, 6, 14, 16, 18, 124, 131, 141; reference to "niggers" in, 4, 53, 56–57, 59–60, 65–66; relevancy to modern times, 135; signature themes, 2; source material for, 51; theological motives in, 119–20; white characters, 19, 23–24, 126; "Wildcat," 10, 45–46; *Wise Blood*, 73, 75–76, 141, 142. *See also individual fictional stories*
O'Connor's letters: to Elizabeth Ames, 76; to Cecil Dawkins, 75, 90–91; description of the house, 65; to Thomas Gossett, 61; to Elizabeth Hester, 4, 38, 40, 59, 65, 75, 91, 96, 100; humor and jokes in, 53–54, 55, 65, 66; to Maryat Lee, 3, 18–20, 25, 38, 50, 51–56, 65, 86, 92, 99, 130; to Robie Macauley, 73; to James McCown, 62; omissions in, 55, 56, 65; publication of, 4, 5, 63; recollection of bus incident, 40; reference to contemporary events, 36, 37, 38; reference to illness, 99, 100; reference to Ku Klux Klan, 50; reference to "niggers," 4, 53, 56, 58, 59–60, 65–66; scholarly studies of, 4–5; to William Sessions, 20, 126; to Richard Stern, 38, 54, 55; stories about black people, 64, 65; theme of South as a better place, 55; thoughts about race, 49, 65; unpublished, 4–6
O'Connor's views and opinions: about African Americans, 11, 19, 64, 131; about Muhammad Ali, 52; about James Baldwin, 51–52; about Christian poet, 89; about civil rights movement, 7, 81; about Civil War, 128; about Dorothy Day, 82; about free will, 141; about Gossett's work, 62; about Hawthorne's fiction, 126; about Martin Luther King, 52; about liberal integrationists, 82; about loss of "manners," 21–22; about race, 3–5, 6, 9, 10, 21–22, 24, 34–35, 40, 44, 57, 63, 65, 77, 95, 141–42; about Eudora Welty, 37–38
Old Dudley (character): miscommunication with black man, 131; racist attitudes, 45;

relationship between Rabie and, 1, 27, 29, 45, 120, 121; social and cultural background, 25–26
Old Gabriel (character), 45–46
Omi, Michael, 16, 23
Osborne, William, 84
Other/Otherness, 112–13, 120

Pemberton, John Stith, 129
Percy, Walker, 62; *Signposts in a Strange Land*, 39
Perreault, Jeanne, 112, 116
physical body, 10, 110
*Playing in the Dark: Whiteness and the Literary Imagination* (Morrison), 10, 15, 66, 97–98, 101, 123, 124
*Plessy vs. Ferguson*, 15
poet: as a blind man, metaphor of, 89
*Prayer Journal*, 71–72

Rabie (character), 1, 26, 27, 29, 45, 120–21
race(s): in American literature, 3, 97, 125; development of the concept of, 11, 16–17, 61; idea of equality between, 141–42; revelation and, 89–96; social relations and, 17; theological concepts of, 10
racial code, 9–10, 21–22, 23, 44
racial miscommunication, 134
racism: in American culture, 9; color-blindness and, 42; definition of, 7, 23; historical usage of the term, 16; idolatry of, 87–89; repressed, 42; of southern Christians, 39, 63; theological view of, 69; white people and, 7–8
Ransom, John Crowe, 56, 57
Rayber (character), 41–42, 43, 44
"Revelation" (O'Connor): as allegory of O'Connor's conversion, 95; depiction of racist thoughts, 3; plot, 89–90, 94–95; procession of the Communion of Saints, 95; racial theme, 17; reference to "niggers," 57–58; scholarly analysis of, 10; visions in, 94–95; "white trash" character, 63–64
Roberts, Diane, 115
Rosa (character), 46–47
Ruby Turpin (character): attack on, 90; incident in doctor's office, 131; interaction with black people, 93–94; interrogation by Jesus, 58; personality of, 89, 90; prototype of, 91–92; racism of, 3, 91; reference to "niggers," 58; self-discovery of, 96; visions of, 94–95, 96; wrestling match with God, 90

Rummel, Joseph, Archbishop of New Orleans, 85

Schroeder, Michael, 37
Second Vatican Council, 86
segregation: Catholic Church's attitudes toward, 10, 84, 85; in education system, 20; establishment of, 15; opposition to, 61, 62; on public buses, 21; roots of, 18
Sessions, William, 71, 126
Shackleford, D. Dean, 32, 105
Shakespeare, William, 130
slavery: black women's bodies and, 101–2, 115; Catholic Church and, 83
Smith, Barbara Herrnstein, 10, 67
social body, 10, 102, 110, 111, 118
Southern cabala, 22
southern culture: attitude to black people, 62; civil rights movement and, 39–40; code of manners, 59, 76, 132; social relations, 21–22, 23
speech act theory, 10, 67
Srigley, Susan, 138
Stefanic, Jean, 43
Stern, Richard, 38, 54, 55
Styron, William, 59
Sykes, John D., Jr., 130

T. C. Tanner (character): death of, 2, 31, 33, 122, 123; homesickness of, 30, 31, 33; image of black body and, 121–22, 123; love of, 34; personality of, 28; prototype of, 2; racial pride of, 29–30; relationship with Coleman, 2, 25–26, 27, 28–29, 30–31, 34, 120; threatened identity of, 2
Teilhard de Chardin, Pierre, 10, 80–81
Till, Emmet, 21

*Violent Bear It Away, The* (O'Connor): characters, 41, 135–36; communion of Saints, 138, 139; Eucharistic vision, 139; literary award for, 129; moments of communion, 140, 141, 142; plot, 136–38; portrayal of failure and hope, 11; relationships between the living and the dead, 138; religious images, 137–38

Walker, Alice, 13–14, 15, 23, 24, 34, 48
Welty, Eudora: O'Connor's criticism of, 37–38, 102; response to Medgar Evers's murder, 37, 39, 55; use of word "nigger" by, 58

whiteness: of American Catholic Church, 87; in American fiction, 34, 126; *vs.* blackness, 8; colonial idea of, 60; dimensions of, 34; discovery of, 15; studies of, 66. *See also* critical whiteness studies
white supremacy myth, 18
Whitt, Margaret Early, 36, 37, 38, 40
Williams, Melvin, 6, 15
Winant, Howard, 16, 23

Wood, Ralph: critique of O'Connor's fiction, 7, 15, 26, 45, 67, 116; on O'Connor's racial ideas, 77, 81–82; on racial crisis, 20; on use of the word "nigger," 59; "Where Is the Voice Coming From? Flannery O'Connor on Race," 67, 70

Yaddo artists' community, 72, 73
Yeats, W. B., 6

ANGELA ALAIMO O'DONNELL is a professor, writer, and poet at Fordham University and the Associate Director of Fordham's Curran Center for American Catholic Studies. Among her recent books are *Flannery O'Connor: Fiction Fired by Faith* (Liturgical, 2015) and *Andalusian Hours: Poems from the Porch of Flannery O'Connor* (Paraclete, 2020).

Lightning Source UK Ltd.
Milton Keynes UK
UKHW012004180521
383946UK00001B/63